"Coaching gains a great deal of depth when it
doxes of human existence and learns to work
tions of human existence in a philosophica!
introductory book Yannick Jacob shows you

    – **Professor Emmy van Deurzen, PhD,** ᴍ.. ⱼ..,
    CPsychol, FBACP, UKCPF, HCPCreg, author of 17 books
    including *Existential Perspectives on Coaching* and
    Principal at the New School of Psychotherapy
    and Counselling, UK

"Trained by the best in existential therapy and influenced by the leaders
in existential positive psychology or second wave positive psychology (PP2.0), Yannick Jacob's book makes a unique contribution to the
coaching profession by combining the depth of existential philosophy
and the clarity and optimism of PP2.0. Personally, I firmly believe that
all coaches, whether they are in life coaching or positive executive
coaching, can benefit from Yannick's book for its refreshing positive
approach to an ancient existential problem. Therefore, I highly recommend this little gem to both novice and seasoned coaches."

    – **Dr Paul T. P. Wong,** President, International Network on
    Personal Meaning; Originator of Existential Positive
    Psychology and Integrative Meaning Therapy

"Coaching unsurprisingly is often fixated with goal focused conversations. But growth can happen through insight, understanding and
meaning. Existential approaches allow us the grace, space and time to
be with clients as they journey through these aspects of their life towards
meaning and purpose. This book provides an outstanding insight into
existential coaching from one of coaching's new rising stars."

    – **Professor Jonathan Passmore,** University of Evora,
    Portugal, and Henley Business School, UK

"Yannick Jacob is a true pioneer, intellectually and practically, in
exploring the fertile ground at the intersection of positive psychology,
existential philosophy, and coaching. This book is a wonderful distil-
lation of his thinking and expertise, touching skilfully and insightfully
upon many important topics, and will be an excellent and inspiring
resource for both scholars and practitioners."

    – **Dr Tim Lomas,** author of 8 books including *The Positive Power*
    of Negative Emotions, The Happiness Dictionary and *Second Wave*
    Positive Psychology: Embracing the Dark Side of Life

"Existential themes have always been at the heart of coaching – after all, we're all human and, coaching, whatever its focus, deals with the strangely cognitive, meaning-making, mortality-aware beast that is the human! Many coaches, though, shy away from looking at existential themes, often wrongly assuming, or even fearing, that deeper issues of meaning, purpose and our confrontation with being human, are best left to the therapist. Yannick is part of a rapidly growing movement of coaches who disagree with this dichotomy and recognise that coaching is always about being human and cannot escape the gravitational pull of the existential givens. In this book, Yannick brings to life the ideas and practices of existential coaching in a way that will allow any coach, new or seasoned, to begin feeling their way into fresh territory or to give language and theory to practices they have naturally been drawn to. A valuable and much needed book for the coaching world."

– **Nick Bolton,** Founder & CEO, Animas Centre for Coaching

"I see so many people who are struggling with problems around meaning and purpose nowadays, it's almost epidemic. That's why great coaching can't shy away from addressing existential concerns and has to deal with them in a hands-on and down-to-earth manner. This is exactly what Yannick is doing with his existential coaching and I'm so glad he finally got to put all of his knowledge and experience together into this work. Bravo!"

– **Seph Fontane Pennock,** co-founder, Positive Psychology Program

"This is an insightful and enlightening introduction to the emerging discipline of existential coaching thoughtfully presented by a passionate and courageous practitioner."

– **Professor Christian van Nieuwerburgh,** Executive Director of Growth Coaching International; Professor of Coaching and Positive Psychology, University of East London, UK

"As long as I can remember, I have been drawn to the idea that the world would be so much better if people truly and deeply contemplated what their lives are really all about. When I started researching meaning, purpose, and existential matters, I found out that, actually, people often freak out if you ask them what their lives are all about! To confront people with such a huge, boundless question can create uncertainty, doubt, even fear. People want to have some sense of safety when diving into these most deep of questions. *An Introduction to Existential Coaching* squarely provides a beautiful solution to this conundrum. By showing how the action-oriented structure of coaching can be used to help people celebrate, rather than fear, uncertainty, this wonderful book shows coaches and other practitioners how to cultivate the inspiration and safety people need to explore and give birth to the best their lives can be about."

> – **Michael F. Steger, PhD,** founding director, Center for Meaning and Purpose, Colorado State University, USA

"Yannick does more than give a deep, new meaning to coaching, he also provides a challenging and refreshing way to view our own existence and purpose. Reading this challenged the way I think and behave, and though uncomfortable, will likely change how I coach. This book will be recommended to everyone on our team."

> – **Bill Eckstrom,** speaker, author and President, EcSell Institute

"I love the existential approach. It takes you deeper into your personal meaning in life and the experience of authenticity. Combine it with a strong foundation of coaching and you get an inspiring marriage. This book is a wonderful reflection of that marriage, providing you with a clear understanding of both theory and practice within existential coaching. Whether you seek personal transformation, or the coaching of others, this book would be an essential tool in your tool-box."

> – **Itai Ivtzan, PhD,** Associate Professor, Naropa University, USA; author of *Awareness is Freedom: The Adventure of Psychology and Spirituality*

"Yannick Jacob's book delivers on its promise to introduce his understanding of existential coaching to a wider readership. The writing is clear and accessible and Jacob's enthusiasm for the subject is evident throughout."

> – **Professor Ernesto Spinelli,** ES Associates, UK

"This is a must-read for any coach, new or experienced, who wants to begin to learn more about the existential approach to their craft. Yannick's experience, expertise and passion for the topic shine through, as he presents the fundamentals of existential coaching, whilst also giving his insights into the industry as a whole."

> – **Sasha van Deurzen-Smith,** Existential Coach and Programme Leader of the MA Existential Coaching at the New School of Psychotherapy and Counselling, UK

"This book is a valuable resource to coaches seeking to go deeper with their clients. The book not only identifies the complex web of existential concerns experienced by clients, but also provides practical coaching approaches that help clients to meaningfully examine the underlying drivers of their behaviours. The book has a secondary goal of helping the reader to identify existential themes in their own life, thus refining their coaching offering."

— **Richard Thorby, ACC, MBA(IMD),** leadership coach

"In his book, *An Introduction to Existential Coaching,* Yannick Jacob gives us an excellent insight into and positioning of this important philosophical yet incredibly relevant approach. Existential questions are at the core of many presenting issues in coaching and this book will greatly deepen how you support psychological wellbeing in your client. The existential inquiry questions throughout the book create a rich toolkit for self-reflection and for working with others. The book prompted me to reflect on what I do and how I do it and reading it was an excellent way to reflect on my current boundaries of practice. I highly recommend this book for seasoned and new coaches alike and I will be adding it to my practitioner's library. Thank you for writing this important introductory volume."

— **Dr Magdalena Bak-Maier,** High Performance Coach and Heart & Mind Integration Method Pioneer

"Coaching is often seen as a way to support clients in achieving their goals. In today's complex and uncertain world, there's an urgent need for coaching to help clients open up, and explore, the bigger questions of life and existence, and to find ways to live with the uncertainty of life. This book is an important contribution to our profession as it seeks to address the deeper concerns of the world in which we live and work."

— **Aboodi Shabi,** leadership coach

"Existential writers are not known for their brevity. In contrast, Yannick Jacob has managed to distil an enormous amount of existential philosophy and coaching practice into this short volume. This is the book I wish I had when I first began working as a coach many years ago. It opens the door to the world of existential coaching and maps out a landscape that any coach, whether experienced or new to the world of coaching, can explore. The author's own authenticity is there on every page, sharing personal insights and questions to reflect upon. Overall, a wonderful introduction to existential coaching, which I thoroughly enjoyed reading – it reminded me why I coach."

– Billy Byrne, executive coach and leadership
development specialist

"I suspect that the concept of existential coaching is still, by and large, met with bewilderment in the coaching community. Yet, this approach has much to offer, especially at this time of great uncertainties, so a primer on existential coaching is timely indeed. Jacob's book is easy to read and well structured, offering a step by step introduction to this field that even those without previous knowledge and experience may find useful and may be encouraged to incorporate some of its elements into their practice."

– Dr Nash Popovic, co-author of Personal Consultancy:
A Model for Integrating Coaching and Counselling;
founder of the first postgraduate programme in
Integrative Counselling and Coaching

"Existential questions and yearnings are as old as humanity itself, and it seems that the fast-paced, digital, and global twenty-first century presents its own unique set of challenges. In the face of the uncertainty and instability of our times, mental health professionals are in need to address pressing existential concerns in an accessible yet profound manner. In this inspiring book, Yannick Jacob takes us through a journey of self-discovery and offers a blueprint for living a full and meaningful life. The book weaves together key principles, insightful reflections and hands-on interventions into a comprehensive, integrative and approachable framework. Direct, clear and well-researched, this book presents valuable ideas and engaging practical tools for coaches, therapists, educators, students, and essentially any human being striving to reach increased self-understanding and growth."

– Dr Pninit Russo-Netzer, Diplomate Clinician in Logotherapy;
co-editor of Meaning in Positive and Existential
Psychology and Clinical Perspectives on Meaning:
Positive and Existential Psychotherapy

"Yannick's book fills a significant gap in the existential coaching literature in that it can be readily applied in the organisational space and is accessible to everyone including those just beginning to explore what existential and/or coaching means. Knowing Yannick's commitment and passion to existentialism and coaching I can truly say that we are fortunate he has given his energy and time to creating a work that will hopefully widen the understanding and practice of existential thinking in the coaching space. It will be an excellent resource for any coaching training programmes of the future as well as to those experienced coaches (in house or independent) who have often wondered what existential coaching is and how to practically apply it to their client work."

— **Angela Jopling,** leadership coach and coaching supervisor, BrightStar Executive Coaching

"Having been described as a quiet mover and shaker in the field of coaching psychology in the UK, I am perhaps well placed as a witness to the innovations (or lack of them) in this field. However, just occasionally one's belief in human potential is revived through encountering an inspirational and life affirming read. Yannick's new text does just that. I enjoyed reading about his own journey and how this has translated into his practice and teaching. He models the existential commitment in every word and does not shy away from engaging with the big questions. It is a book that is destined to become a 'go to' title for any practitioner wanting their minds opened, not only to the essentials of existential coaching, but to how to live and work with courage, passion and authentically in tough times. I have reviewed many books and articles in this field, yet none has given me so much pleasure as this. Writing this endorsement has been a gift and I am reminded throughout of the words of the poet Rumi, who said: 'Let the beauty of what you love, be what you do.' Yannick's contribution exemplifies this and more."

— **Margaret Chapman-Clarke,** positive psychologist, existential coach; editor, *Mindfulness in the Workplace: An Evidence-Based Approach to Improving Wellbeing and Maximising Performance*

"Yannick's book, *An Introduction to Existential Coaching*, brought me back to the excitement I felt when I first discovered the existential approach. Thank you! I've always appreciated anyone who can wrangle the words of something as seemingly illusive as existential coaching. Not only did Yannick make these concepts accessible, but enjoyable. I smiled almost the entire time reading the book. The only time I didn't have a wide grin on my face was when I got to the marketing chapter. During that chapter I was nodding my head in agreement. I think any coach who is serious about growing their business will understand that reaction. Yannick's style brings to the surface, in an authentic way, brain tingling questions, valuable ideas, and important challenges. He successfully integrates complex philosophical underpinnings with practical implications for coaching, which makes the book accessible to new and experienced coaches alike."

– **Linda DeLuca,** author, *An Exploration of the Existential Orientation to Coaching*

"Reframing existentialism from its dark associations to something that is profoundly empowering – this is not an easy task! Yannick excels at unpacking big ideas in a playful, analytical and down-to-earth way and communicate practical applications in the coaching setting. He walks the talk – you can almost hear his challenging curiosity and passion for life speak through the pages – encouraging and reminding to reflect, open our ears to the ephemeral nature of moments and to embrace the rawness and uncertainty of life as a source for meaning. A mindset of aliveness. This is a bold and compelling message – not just for the coach reader and their clients but also for humanity."

– **Georgie Nightingall,** life coach, trainer, speaker, philosophy teacher; founder, Trigger Conversations

"Existential ideas and therapeutic approaches are concerned with questions about the nature of human existence, inviting us to reflect critically and creatively about some of the key challenges of our lives, including: finding purpose and meaning in life, facing uncertainty, crisis and mortality, taking responsibility, living authentically, belonging and more. In this inspiring and thought-provoking book, Yannick Jacob skilfully demonstrates how these ideas can be incorporated into the practice of coaching, to reflect on clients' life choices, concerns and challenges, and help them achieve their desired transformations. With a strong, practice-based approach that draws on the author's vast experience and the existing research in this area, this book provides a thorough, engaging and creative guide to existential coaching, and is an essential reading for all coaches, scholars and trainees."

– **Dr Rona Hart,** Programme Leader, MSc Applied Positive Psychology, University of East London, UK

"As a practitioner of existential coaching I welcome Yannick Jacob's book very much. It is a thorough, inspiring and well written introduction to the principles of existential coaching as well as the philosophical stance, attitudes and competences necessary for coaches who would like to work with other people in this life-affirming way. Even though the topic is complex and not always easy to grasp Yannick writes in a light and motivating way, connecting with the reader by means of important questions for reflection throughout the book. My hope is that this book will help more coaches take up the existential approach and thus develop competences that can truly help people with the work towards living more authentic and hopefully better lives."

– **Anne Kongsted Krum,** senior consultant, Cabi; existential coach, DilemmaCoaching and Stress-Profilen.dk

"Reading these pages will transform both yours and your client's lives. Like many freshly qualified coaches, I too felt the need to niche after completing my training. My search for a specialty began and ended at Yannick's training weekend in existential coaching. This book strikes the same delicate balance as the course. Yannick's welcoming conversational-style invitation to explore is underpinned by a well-researched foundation, offering a life-changing opportunity for coaches and clients alike. Yannick makes this emerging and often misunderstood area of coaching accessible for anyone seeking to dive deeper into life's unknowns. Simple, easy to read, yet profoundly needed today."

– **Marcie Boyer,** existential life coach; author, *What I Know about Jumping: Real Life Lessons on Finding the Courage to Make Major Life Change*

"If I were not an existential practitioner already, I would want to become one after reading this book! Yannick has written an accessible introduction into existential coaching. He explains difficult concepts and complex phenomena in simple words. He embeds the unique position of the existential coach within the wider field of coaching in general. Yannick's passion for his job shines through his words and personal examples. The author has a bridge-building approach: he is both personal and relational, informed by existential philosophy and positive psychology, both pragmatic and informed by research. Building bridges is of utmost importance in our era of disintegration of people helping professions. This book is timely, as the coaching discipline seems to have fallen into the grip of superficial solution-focused approaches, but Yannick shows the importance and the appeal of basing the practice of coaching on existential foundations. He introduces key concepts from existential philosophy, and his exercises invite the reader to engage actively with the concepts. This book offers readers the first simple stepping stones on the complex road towards existential work."

– **Dr Joel Vos, PhD,** researcher and lecturer at Metanoia Institute; leader, professional doctorate, Existential Psychotherapy and Counselling at the New School of Psychotherapy and Counselling, UK; author, *Meaning in Life: An Evidence-Based Handbook for Practitioners*

"The domain of start-ups represents a special and unique context for existential coaching. Start-ups by nature are fast-paced, action-oriented, and much of the learning is on the job. Knowing has become obsolete. How we behave when *not knowing* has become the new currency. Many people show up for work blind and groping in the dark. Many eyes have not yet opened to behold the surprising sights of true leadership in the modern workforce. The existential leader is the new Holy Grail. The coaching space that Yannick lays out allows this leader to emerge and thrive."

– **Matthew Laffer,** Founder & CEO, Goalspriing

An Introduction to Existential Coaching

In *An Introduction to Existential Coaching* Yannick Jacob provides an accessible and practical overview of existential thought and its value for coaches and clients.

Jacob begins with an introduction to coaching as a powerful tool for change, growth, understanding and transformation before exploring existential philosophy and how it may be integrated into coaching practice. The book goes on to examine key themes in existentialism and how they show up in the coaching space, including practical models as well as their application to organisations and leadership. Jacob concludes by evaluating ethical dimensions of working existentially and offers guidance on how to establish an existential coaching practice, including how to gain clients and build relationships with strategic partners. With reflective questions, exercises, interventions and activities throughout, *An Introduction to Existential Coaching* will be invaluable for anyone wanting to live and work at greater depth or to succeed as an existential coach.

Accessibly written and with a wide selection of references and resources, *An Introduction to Existential Coaching* is a vital guide for coaches in training as well as an inspiring addition to the repertoir of experienced practitioners. It serves academics and students to understand existential philosophy and allows professionals with coaching responsibilities to access more meaningful conversations.

Yannick Jacob is a coach, trainer, supervisor, mediator and change agent in private practice as well as the former Programme Leader of the MSc Coaching Psychology at the University of East London, UK. He works with coaches, leaders and anybody who considers themselves to be in a position of great responsibility. Yannick believes in balance, clarity, helping people think and developing the courage to live across the full spectrum of human experience as the pathway to happiness.

An Introduction to Existential Coaching

How Philosophy Can Help Your Clients Live with Greater Awareness, Courage and Ownership

Yannick Jacob

Routledge
Taylor & Francis Group

LONDON AND NEW YORK

First published 2019
by Routledge
2 Park Square, Milton Park, Abingdon, Oxon OX14 4RN

and by Routledge
52 Vanderbilt Avenue, New York, NY 10017

Routledge is an imprint of the Taylor & Francis Group, an informa business

British Library Cataloguing-in-Publication Data
A catalogue record for this book is available from the British Library

Library of Congress Cataloging-in-Publication Data
Names: Jacob, Yannick, 1983- author.
Title: An introduction to existential coaching : how philosophy
    can help your clients live with greater awareness, courage and
    ownership / Yannick Jacob.
Description: 1 Edition. | New York : Routledge, 2019. | Includes
    bibliographical references and index.
Identifiers: LCCN 2018053861 (print) | LCCN 2018061459 (ebook) |
    ISBN 9780429432330 (Master eBook) | ISBN 9780429778681
    (Adobe Reader) | ISBN 9780429778667 (Mobipocket) | ISBN
    9780429778674 (ePub) | ISBN 9781138362048 (hardback) |
    ISBN 9780367139995 (pbk.) | ISBN 9780429432330 (ebk)
Subjects: LCSH: Personal coaching. | Positive psychology.
Classification: LCC BF637.P36 (ebook) | LCC BF637.P36 J33 2019
    (print) | DDC 158.3—dc23
LC record available at https://lccn.loc.gov/2018053861

ISBN: 978-1-138-36204-8 (hbk)
ISBN: 978-0-367-13999-5 (pbk)
ISBN: 978-0-429-43233-0 (ebk)

Typeset in Times New Roman
by Swales & Willis Ltd, Exeter, Devon, UK

Contents

Figures and tables

Figures

Tables

Acknowledgments

I cannot possibly mention (or indeed even count) the people who have had an influence on this book. Those of you who have met me will know that I have quite an inquisitive and curious mind, and so I want to thank those of you I've been in contact with in some way or another for sharing your stories and experiences, living your life the way you do or challenging me on my views and opinions.

I am particularly grateful to my wife Nelly, who never gets tired of exploring and elevating my worldview in the most loving and passionate way and whose rich psychoanalytic training and experience allows me to look at my philosophy and practice in ever-growing ways. Sharing my journey with you is the best thing that ever happened to me and I have a feeling that many more books will carry your name.

I want to thank Dr Nash Popovic, who has been a great mentor and became a valued friend along my journey of exploring positive psychology through a critical lens and developing my own approach to integrative coach-therapy practice. Without Nash I may not have made the effort to enter academia in the way that I did and this book would look, feel and sound very different. Thank you, Nash!

I would like to thank my parents whole-heartedly for their incredible support, for putting up with my insatiable curiosity and not just accepting, but encouraging me to stand up for what I believe in and courageously follow my own path in this world, regardless of social norms or how they themselves may have felt about it. I cannot thank you enough!

To all the coaches that have passed through my teaching, training and supervision spaces, I probably learn as much from you as I pass on and it is through our deep conversations, open engagement and considered challenges that this book has grown into what it is today.

I would like to express my gratitude and deep respect for Nick Bolton, who was an instrumental part in the realisation of this book and gave me free reign to design my first training course on the subject and the opportunity as well as the encouragement to write the first version of this book. My time within the Animas team and wider community has shaped my training style in a way that felt like coming home and I will always call Animas my spiritual home when it comes to the way you train your coaches.

Many thanks to Monica Hanaway who has not only been an instrumental part of my coaching journey by breathing life into the first MA in Existential Coaching together with Emmy van Deurzen, but has subsequently also trained me as a mediator for existentially informed conflict resolution at Regent's University and provided ongoing developmental support and encouragement well beyond her various job descriptions. I am so thankful for your considered foreword and for contributing so much to the existential approach.

Extended thanks to all the scholars, writers, researchers and practitioners who are part of the second wave of positive psychology, which in essence aims to integrate existential themes into the science that I had so fallen in love with but found to be incomplete in the context of human lived experience. Thanks to Paul Wong, who has encouraged me since the day I first met him and whose writing put into words what I had been practicing at the time but could not quite formulate yet, and my colleagues at the University of East London, Itai Ivtzan, Tim Lomas, Kate Hefferon for their PP2.0 work, and also Rona Hart, William Pennington and the whole MAPPCP team for their continued inspiration and love for spreading knowledge. Special thanks also to Christian van Nieuwerburgh and Aneta Tunariu, who trusted me with the Programme Lead of the MSc Coaching Psychology, which kick-started my academic career and opened many doors. I still hope we will be able to run my "Introduction to Positive Existential Coaching" module in due time.

I'd like to thank my brother Marcus for the many opportunities to face my own mortality in and outside of a range of ski resorts across the world. These experiences and the reflections they've triggered along the way are a never-ending source of existential material.

Special shout out to my "sister" Mel, who has been there for me whenever life had something to throw at me, no matter what. You're the most fragile solid rock I know and I love you.

Jason Silva, thank you for bringing positive existential thought into the world in such an engaging way and modern format. Your films allow those who watch them to dive deeper into their own human experience with an infectious positive attitude and the same childlike curiosity I can sense in myself. We should be friends!

Thanks to all the existential practitioners who have trained or otherwise taught or inspired me, most notably Emmy van Deurzen, Jamie Reed, Angela Jopling, Irvin Yalom, Ernesto Spinelli, David Pullinger, Aboodi Shabi, Tim LeBon, Mo Mandić, Greg Madison as well as all the existential thinkers and writers mentioned in this book.

And lastly I'd like to thank all those who live courageously and with open eyes facing their human condition. Extra brownie points for those embracing it with a smile! You're an inspiration.

Foreword

We live in uncertain times, and we need to find a way to meet that uncertainty in a celebratory way. This lies at the heart of an existential approach. We can learn to welcome and embrace the space and freedom that uncertainty offers to us. Indeed, uncertainty can be seen as a clarion call to creativity. If there is no certainty it is incumbent on us to do something meaningful with the void it provides. Yannick has risen to this challenge in writing *An Introduction to Existential Coaching*, in which he brings together thinking from existentialism, coaching psychology, phenomenology and positive psychology.

It may seem counterintuitive calling on approaches which are more commonly associated with the middle of the last century in the context of something as contemporary as coaching but I strongly believe that an existential approach is highly suited to today's times and challenges, regardless of whether these are personal or professional. I have always been passionate about giving existential and phenomenological thought and practice a place beyond the higher echelons of academia and using in it a practical way, particularly in the world of business, where I consider it has much to offer to today's leaders. This should further extent interest in the approach and this introduction serves as a tangible entry into its foundations and practical applications.

In 2010, I approached Emmy van Deurzen at the New School of Psychotherapy and Counselling, London, to see if she might be interested in offering training in existential coaching. Emmy had established the school on the foundation of existential thought. However, the training offered at that time focused solely on existential psychotherapy. I wanted to build on this important work but take a more business-accessible approach. The initial dialogue led to the development of the MA in Existential Coaching, which is now validated through Middlesex University. This was followed by the publication of the first book that focused specifically on existential coaching, entitled *Existential Perspectives on Coaching* (van Deurzen & Hanaway, 2012). The book explored the philosophy underpinning the approach and contrasted and compared it with other approaches. A long list of contributing authors discussed what an existential approach brought to their already established coaching practice. Since the book was not meant to focus on the specific skills of an existential coach, in 2014, together with Jamie Reed, I wrote *Existential Coaching Skills: The Handbook*, in which we began to address this need. Students who completed the MA and readers of the books have since taken existential ideas into their work with business leaders, established coaches have begun to take an interest in the approach as a different way of working (and thus adding a new offering to their portfolio of services). Those eager to receive coaching training and certification have chosen an existential perspective as their entry point into the profession.

The development of existential coaching is still in its infancy and there is plenty of room for new thought and challenge. I have focused much of my own work on existential leadership, but the approach is equally relevant to personal as well as professional arenas. Increasingly I see growing interest from individuals looking to existential coaching to facilitate their development and from innovative companies keen to make a success of their business in these challenging times. These companies and individuals seek success through establishing meaning whilst staying authentically true to a set of clear values and beliefs.

When establishing the MA I could not have foreseen Yannick, one of its first graduates, passionately embracing the mantle of spreading the word and providing new thinking on the subject. In a short time, Yannick has established training modules in existential coaching and is using the lessons learnt to inform the writing of this book. Participants on his courses, through the questions they have posed and experiences they have shared, have provided a framework for his writing so that any reader, regardless of their individual understanding of what coaching is (and isn't), will find valuable ideas, concepts, skills and tools to inform the way they work.

This book provides an introduction to existential coaching, based on Yannick's own research (Jacob, 2013) as well as the limited amount of resources and literature already existing on the subject. He gives readers new to coaching an idea of what the profession is about and clearly outlines the main existential issues placing them firmly within the coaching context. Uniquely he couples the existential approaches with positive psychology, which offers a positive perspective on a school of thought often portrayed as dark and pessimistic in the public sphere.

The structure of the book is easy to follow, posing questions that those new to existential coaching may bring and then seeking to address these questions in a clear and precise manner which addresses the existential nature of the dilemma at the centre of each question. In addition he gives practical encouragement to those wishing to start an existential coaching practice including a section on how to get clients and develop a flourishing practice. For those working as existential coaches, consultants and trainers, there is a question as to how overt we are about our philosophical approach. Many people carry negative assumptions about the nature of existential thought which may make it harder for an existential coach to attract a significant number of clients. Yet, it is essential that those of us who do embrace and practice the approach make it better known and understood, so that it may take its place as a valid and valued coaching offering. Yannick's book offers an opportunity to begin to understand this exciting approach to coaching.

Monica Hanaway, 2018

References

Hanaway, M., & Reed, J. (2014). *Existential Coaching Skills: The Handbook.* Henley-on-Thames: Corporate Harmony.

Jacob, Y.U. (2013). Exploring Boundaries of Existential Coaching. Master's thesis. Retrieved from www.academia.edu/8376861/Exploring_Boundaries_ of_Existential_Coaching.

van Deurzen, E., & Hanaway, M. (2012). *Existential Perspectives on Coaching.* Basingtoke, UK: Palgrave Macmillan.

Preface

A young toddler is one of the most fearless beings that I have ever encountered. My second nephew, fuelled by his recently added skill of using his legs in new and very efficient ways, has now reached the age of exploring furiously and without any noticeable boundaries to his curiosity. All babies are naturally curious. But as we grow up we learn to be fearful through our experiences and upbringing. Some people choose to retreat into what they already know, a safe space, others seek novelty courageously (and sometimes recklessly), despite the risks and in the face of great rewards.

Now, curiosity and a keen interest in the world has always been one of my primary driving forces and somehow I have managed to preserve this instinct for three and a half decades. I believe it is important to explore, to learn, to grow, to develop, to understand, to ponder and to make sense of the world; to change, to discover, to connect loose ends and acquire different perspectives as to integrate them into the greater whole. As Socrates famously stated: "The unexamined life is not worth living", which ironically led to his death by execution following his trial for impiety and corrupting the youth in his quest for truth and exploration.

My own curiosity has also led to many deaths (read: endings). Toys got abandoned, hobbies were dropped for more interesting new ones, books were left unread and I fell out of touch with friends as I immersed myself in new relationships. Many relationships broke because I longed for something new and exciting. Many a time I have caused myself and others great suffering as I found myself asking the challenging questions, explore a little too deep, be a bit too honest or get used to what I have and wanting something more or different. Living life in this way is not easy and it took me some time to realise what's going on.

History is full of stories of people who fought hard to bury new developments in an effort to protect the status quo. We like things to stay as they are when they are good (for us or our group). And yet we tend to get depressed and bored when things stay the same for too long, no matter how good they were initially perceived. As human beings, we adapt; a great blessing and a challenging curse. I most certainly enjoy a good time, but something I learned about myself is that I seem to adapt much quicker than others (my top character strength according to the Gallup Strengths Finder but, as I had experienced, also a burden in many ways). We know today that due to this human characteristic we are stepping in a hedonic treadmill and that the goalpost constantly shifts upwards as we tread through life, and yet the world is full of people who are constantly chasing comfort and happiness (read: pleasant emotions) as if it were sustainable and in the process neglect to appreciate what meaning and fulfilment lies in embracing the whole spectrum of what life has to offer. I appreciate that this is predominantly a "Western" problem and it is to no surprise that much of the original existential literature spawned in the affluent conditions of Europe. There simply isn't enough time to think deeply about questions of existence when you are busy surviving. However, I believe, and then experienced through the stories of the people I've met across all walks of life, from the 1% to those trying to survive to varying degrees of success, that the thoughts and ideas of these early existentialists are worth the renaissance they are currently experiencing.

While I experienced a fair amount of psychological torment and existential challenge in my life so far, I was lucky enough to be raised by parents who did not just allow or endure, but actively encouraged me to pursue a career that I would enjoy, something I could be passionate about and interested in, something authentic, regardless of how it was judged by society. They knew that passion breeds commitment, and that commitment breeds success. And they knew that psychological wellbeing is far more important than financial wealth. They would have probably slept a lot better initially had I stepped into a "safe" career choice such as medicine or law, but they seemed to embrace the discomfort of having their son hang around some dubious people, engage in strange creative practices and then travel across the continent to study psychology, and the then completely unknown science of happiness and wellbeing, applied positive psychology, in particular. By the time I graduated from the second Master's programme in the world created by Ilona Boniwell at the University of East London, there were no job ads looking for positive psychologists and my keen interest in deep philosophical questions about the nature of life had not exactly led me to pave financially promising avenues. That is until I discovered coaching as the seemingly ideal way to follow my psychotherapeutic interests in an authentic and efficient way, and then (to my parent's delight) learned about its subsequent boom across pretty much all industries. It was then that I knew I was onto something that was in line with my values, in demand (as long as people lived among other people) and something that would keep me engaged and interested for the rest of my life as well as well-paid if I played my cards right.

As an introvert (who has learned to *do* extroversion) I had always had a craving for deep thought and my dearest friends were those who happily sat down to talk for hours about why people do the things they do and how we can make sense of this strange world. Not surprisingly I had been flirting with analysis, psychotherapy and counselling during my undergraduate degree in psychology. As a questioning rebel however I was not impressed by the extent of restrictions, guidelines, boundaries and limitations imposed by what I perceived as the same status quo protectors who had gotten rid of Socrates. I yearned for an approach to working with people that would allow me to be who I am, grant me the freedom to do what I want and what I deemed most helpful, a way of working that would not box me into a specific category of "aaah, right, you're one of those".

Most importantly, I wanted to offer a space which people would seek out *before* they felt they were no longer able to cope with life and in desperate need of help. I knew that exploring our inner and outer worlds in the context of a trusting and respectful relationship can be highly therapeutic and I wondered why most people would wait until something bad happened before they went on a quest to find out who they are and what makes them tick. There is no one-size-fits-all formula for how to do life or for why you do the things you do (even though that fantasy seems to sell formidably well among people who yearn for simplicity). I had thought many things through in my life and had gained a valuable range of perspectives on a variety of small and big issues. Being curious about and exploring in-depth what people get upset or excited about opened up an appreciation of there not being a right or wrong, just different. And who was I to judge how others choose to live their lives. After all, I valued my freedom, so I had to respect others' too.

Spending my university days and early career oscillating between sophisticated academic debates at the forefront of positive psychology and immersing myself in the fun-loving, down-to-earth, multinational creative scene of East London's famous artist quarter Hackney Wick in combination with a privileged upbringing in Germany and many friends who would go on to work in lucrative industries such as finance or business consulting, I got to know a broad spectrum of people at considerable depth and learned what they consider a good life, what they struggle with on a daily basis, how they make meaning in their lives, what they believe in and how they think life should be lived. I also noticed that much of what other people struggled with and tried to make disappear I had learned to appreciate. I had developed a mindset that embraced uncertainty. I had learned to value the feeling of being nervous from not knowing as the *stuff* that makes life exciting. I had realised that the best stories I told, heard or read were about challenge and overcoming hardship. The works of art I most connected with, enjoyed or had been most proud of producing had been created out of and inspired by dilemmas, hardship, uncertainty, the search for meaning, life-and-death situations, endings, difficult questions and the challenging exploration of who, what and why we are. And while I felt the same anxiety facing those questions, it seemed that my attitude towards these feelings, my mindset and the story I told myself made all the difference.

Positive psychology (empirically exploring the positive side of human psychology) had equipped me with a particular lens on what lay beyond. So naturally I wanted to be a practitioner who is able to work across the whole spectrum of what people experience along the journey. I had seen successful business owners, shiny Instagram account holders and those who seemingly have everything they could wish for in life, be profoundly unhappy; and I had seen those with no belongings, little opportunity and Sisyphus-like weights on their shoulders flourish and appreciate life. Stereotypical life coaches and positive psychologists though often seemed to be way too positive and failed to appreciate that life will throw you a bunch of curved balls, give you plenty of lemons and never ends with anybody living happily ever after. Creating knowledge about what is right with people through empirical science is a valuable endeavour, but too many of those applying the science were selling quick fixes and shortcuts to the kind of happiness that I had concluded to be unsustainable.

The second wave of positive psychologists started to integrate the darker side of the spectrum into their research and conceptualisations of happiness. The problem was that this wave had not gained momentum yet and when I graduated from the MAPP programme in early 2010, almost none of the now influential literature of the second wave of positive psychology (e.g. Wong, 2010, 2011; Ivtzan, Lomas, Hefferon & Worth, 2016) had been produced. Equipped with a wealth of scientific knowledge, conceptualisations of psychological wellbeing and happiness, a host of tools and interventions to measure and affect a whole range of different aspects of life and a strong desire to work across the spectrum human lived experience I went on a quest to find an integrative approach to coaching and therapy. I was looking for a way of working that would allow me to go into depth with clients and help them to connect to themselves on a much deeper level than traditional performance coaching was able to, where people could look forward and backwards as they saw fit, to create a space where we can ask the questions that might challenge you to the core but from a position of curiosity and exploration rather than the need to fix an imminent crisis. I wanted to open people's eyes to the beauty of learning to embrace the darker and more challenging sides of our existence at a time when they are well able and freely willing to engage with such questions, not out of necessity or to climb out of a hole. I knew that if I had learned to build existential resilience then others could do that too, well before they would need it as a defence against adversity. What I needed was a framework that acknowledged that the world was a difficult place to be in, that the mere act of living life could be incredibly tough and challenging, even for people in seemingly affluent environments.

And so it was that I found existentialism in an effort to join a training course that would combine elements of coaching and counselling. Not that I would gain a counselling or therapy qualification as it turned out (even though a large part of the literature we digested was from that field), but it was the closest I got to working integrated. And boy am I glad today that I ended up in the world's first cohort of the MA in Existential Coaching, created by Emmy van Deurzen and Monica Hanaway at the New School of Psychotherapy and Counselling, together with a handful of eager learners and a list of tutors longer and more varied than I had ever seen. The mix of science, philosophy and applied practice and in particular the existential framework felt immediately like home. Looking at traditionally often bleak-seeming existential ideas through a positive psychology lens and in the context of coaching was a revelation that slowly but surely (some of this stuff can't be read, it has to be worked through, digested, processed, applied, questioned, reformulated, tested, discussed, let go and re-built from the ground up in a new context) build a solid, yet flexible foundation for working with coaching clients positively within an existential framework. It felt like I had arrived and yet there was something new to discover every day. I was home and at the same time still journeying. I had found a framework for what it means to be human that everybody I talked to was able to connect with (once I managed to translate complex existential ideas into everyday language and experiences) while at the same time being able to draw in tools, interventions, techniques and process from any other approach to working with people that I would see fit and appropriate depending on context. I was free. And I found a niche that I could call home.

And what followed felt like having woken up. Wherever I went, whatever people talked about, any engaging story, film or conversation I heard, the issues that people brought from different areas of their personal or professional lives, were all clearly connected to underlying existential concerns. It was as if I was able to read between the lines. It was not always appropriate to reflect this back but it opened up an understanding of people's concerns and behaviours that I had never experienced this clearly. I started noticing popular business books talking openly about what I knew were existential themes: uncertainty, risk and decision making; authenticity, identity, vulnerability, charisma and courage to be different; crisis, endings, risk, change and challenging the status quo; mindset, resilience, grit; the complexities of relationships, importance of leading with strong values; holding paradox, absurdity and facing dilemmas and not-knowing courageously; leading with backbone and heart in a world that will never be happy ever after with the next crisis just around the corner; the list goes on. And those with an existential mindset and an appreciation of these ideas seemed to have an edge.

The more I read and discussed as well as worked with my own coaching clients (who spanned across all walks of life during this time), the more I felt able to communicate my ideas to others. After I had found my voice and built a strong foundation for my work I started meeting like-minded practitioners and researchers who shared my views. Paul Wong (2010, 2011) had been writing about positive existential psychology, my later colleagues at UEL, particularly Itai Ivtzan and Tim Lomas (Ivtzan et al., 2016), had written about second-wave positive psychology (filled with references to existential themes) and the value of so-called "negative" emotions, Emmy and Monica (van Deurzen & Hanaway, 2012) had brought together a range of practitioners and edited *Existential Perspectives on Coaching* (including the vast majority of those who had been teaching on the course) and Monica together with her colleague Jamie Reed also published a chunky handbook (Hanaway & Reed, 2014), complete with models for application, practical guidelines and a chapter on existential leadership in the context of coaching practice (to be developed into its own volume in the near future). Next to the still new and largely unknown MA in Existential Coaching, Nick Bolton was developing ambitious plans of growing his coaching school Animas into the largest coaching school in the UK and ultimately venturing out into the world. When I found a simple tweet of his mentioning existential coaching a connection was born that a few months later led to me designing and delivering weekend training courses in existential coaching and positive psychology. I learned that Nick's approach was deeply existential and the transformational coaching approach he was teaching at Animas shared a very similar foundation to mine. Through the work with Animas students I realised that there is a real desire both from coaches and clients to explore bigger questions and to go deeper into whatever is being brought into the coaching space. Not everybody is up for working with people in this way or looking at their own existence in more depth, facing their existential challenges, but more and more coaches started to approach me for supervision and training in order to be able to go further professionally and offer a richer service to their clients.

When in 2015 Christian van Nieuwerburgh handed over the programme leadership of the MSc in Coaching Psychology at the University of East London, I found myself exchanging ideas with hundreds of practitioners from a variety of different approaches (MSc Career Coaching, MSc Coaching Psychology, MSc Applied Positive Psychology & Coaching Psychology and the ground-breaking brand new MSc Integrative Coaching and Counselling founded by my colleague, early mentor and now dear friend Nash Popovic). What became clear during these fruitful exchanges, debates, lectures, supervision sessions and watercooler conversations was that nobody knew where exactly the line was between coaching and other helping-by-talking practices, but everybody would inevitably be faced with situations in which they had to make an ethical decision as to how far they were willing, able and allowed to go. I wasn't training coaches who only follow Whitmore's (1992) popular GROW model (Goals, Reality, Options, Way forward), the application of which is often characterized by following a step-by-step process to help somebody improve performance and change behaviour. I was providing a space in which learners had to make difficult decisions in the face of very few clear guidelines as to what is and isn't allowed to be called coaching. In a way, coaching resembled life itself, and there were no clear-cut definitive answers of right and wrong. If you wanted to be a good coach, you had to go through the motions, find out who you are, what you believe in, what you think about human nature, our ability to make changes and what your strengths are and then build your own unique coaching approach around your uniqueness. How far you are able to go with your clients depends on your abilities and beliefs across a wide spectrum, and only through continuous reflective practice, supervision, good ethical standards, authentic and courageous engagement and transparent contracting are you able to navigate through the coaching space with confidence and effectiveness and provide the best service for your clients. An appreciation of the challenging journey ahead and the need to make plenty of difficult decisions to which we cannot know the answers, nor have enough time to think about, and a belief that the only way to do this well is to choose despite not knowing and take responsibility for our actions and inactions, turns out to be appreciated by those who want to get the most out of their time on this planet and to engage as fully as possible in their life and career.

Whether you are a coach or a client (and I believe a good coach will always be both), I hope that this book may be the beginning of a similar journey for you, a journey into better understanding the human condition, embracing your inevitable anxieties and inner conflicts, living courageously and with passion and to engage with your clients and fellow human beings with the empathy that such an understanding entails.

References

Hanaway, M., & Reed, J. (2014). *Existential Coaching Skills: The Handbook*. Henley-on-Thames, UK: Corporate Harmony.

Ivtzan, I., Lomas, T., Worth, P. & Hefferon, K. (2016). *Second Wave Positive Psychology: Embracing the Dark Side of Life*. London: Routledge.

van Deurzen, E., & Hanaway, M. (2012). *Existential Perspectives on Coaching*. Basingtoke, UK: Palgrave Macmillan.

Wong, P.T.P. (2010). What is existential positive psychology? *International Journal of Existential Psychology & Psychotherapy*, 3, 1–10.

Wong, P.T.P. (2011). Positive psychology 2.0: Towards a balanced interactive model of the good life. *Canadian Psychology*, 52(2), 69–81.

Introduction

What this book is about

This book is an introduction to the essentials of existential coaching, a short and tangible introduction that will be ideal as a starting point into learning about the existential approach to coaching and life. It does not attempt to be the final word on the approach or to put forward a specific system for coaching people existentially (though some models and guidelines are put forward for the reader to engage with), but rather it is an opening for you to grasp the framework, understand its core ideas and gather enough tools, details and information in order to go out and start applying what you have learned in your existing coaching practice or in your own life.

I will introduce you the core tenets of coaching, but mostly focus on existential principles, key issues, models and practicalities of existential coaching and offer questions and exercises for you to try out as you play with the concepts. This book aims to build on your existing skills and knowledge (which, believe it or not, you all possess), rather than being a wholesale replacement for other coaching and philosophy books. It introduces the foundational concepts of existential philosophy along with the required aptitudes of this approach so that you can choose to either embrace an existential coaching approach fully or simply let an understanding of the philosophy add to your existing coaching style.

Existential coaching helps people to address those eternal human questions that we all (some more, some less often) sense at a deeper level in our day-to-day lives. Questions like: How can I be happier? What is the meaning of (my) life? How can I be authentic? What's the right thing to do? Is this really all there is to life? What is my purpose? Am I living well?

Another aspect that we share as human beings is that we all face certain inescapable conditions as a result of being human and in the world with others. We have to bear a recurring awareness of our inevitable death and the fact that all things, from the significant to the mundane, will end; we all have to make choices without any certainty of the outcome; we are hard-wired for attachment in a world defined by impermanence; and we are social animals in dire need of connecting to others but at the same time value our individuality and have to live with the fact that nobody can ever fully and truly see us in our entirety. These conditions and others, often called the human givens or the human condition, present unavoidable realities of being alive, confronting us with limitations as well as possibilities. We can feel these strongly, often as a form of anxiety, eeriness, discomfort or dread.

From a coaching perspective, these questions and conditions are often at the core of the everyday challenges that clients bring to us – sometimes implicitly, sometimes explicitly. And while exploring these issues and concerns is not always needed (or perhaps even desired by clients), it is greatly valuable to understand human beings in this way and at times such explorations can have a profound impact, changing the way someone experiences and lives their life. This is particularly true when clients feel incongruent or inauthentic in their lives, where social pressures, the way their identity and worldview was shaped growing up, self-expectation, fears and anxiety create dilemmas and choices that they feel unable, or unwilling, to meet; when we find ourselves in a situation in which we can no longer deny that these givens and paradoxes exist and that living comfortably or happily ever after is simply not an option without deceiving ourselves or investing great energy into keeping up a delusion.

This is where existential coaching has a significant role to play and this book will introduce you to the main tenets.

List of topics

In particular, you will explore:

- A general framework for coaching practice.
- Key differences between existential coaching and other forms of practice.
- Existential ideas and their intellectual origins.
- The four core existential concerns of death, meaninglessness, isolation and freedom, including themes such as time and endings,

choice and decision-making, uncertainty, authenticity, identity and self, the impact of others, the importance of worldviews and beliefs, and how these themes show up in everyday living.

- Psychological defence mechanisms against existential suffering and the concept of "bad faith".
- Existential "solutions".
- How to lay the right foundations with your clients.
- Models and guidelines for existential coaching practice.
- Tools and techniques such as phenomenological inquiry and working with the here-and-now.
- Existential coaching in business and leadership.
- Ethical considerations.
- Integrating existentialism into existing approaches to coaching.
- How to get clients as an existential coach.

By the end of this book you will have an understanding of the existential coaching landscape: where it fits, how it is practised and how it can inform your coaching practice. I hope you will enjoy reading this book and that it will provide value to you and your clients. If at any point you have questions, comments or ideas, I'd be keen on hearing them, so please do not hesitate to reach out.

The purpose of this book

Just as a coach will contract clearly with clients at the outset of their relationship, it is important to me to outline what this book can and cannot do for you. Originally written as an accompaniment to an advanced coach training course I developed and delivered for Animas Centre for Coaching between 2015 and 2018, the aim of this book is to:

- Introduce coaching as a powerful tool for change, growth, understanding and transformation.
- Provide an introduction to existential philosophy (which provides the foundations for the existential approach to coaching).
- Place existential thought into a coaching framework and identify how it may benefit coaching practice.
- Offer some techniques and models that coaches may find useful and that will help them to add existential elements to their practice.
- Grant the reader the freedom to integrate any aspect of this book into your existing life and/or practice rather than providing a one-size-fits-all system of how to coach or live existentially.

Since existentialism has its roots deep inside philosophy, it is intricately linked to a complex web of literature and ideas, and not governed by a unified school of thought or any dominant figure head, this book will:

- Not claim to be a complete guide to existential philosophy. The aim is to open some doors to your thinking and the way you meet people and to provide useful resources and further reading so that the interested coach can immerse him or herself more fully. Developing a full appreciation of existential thought will take more than a short book. It requires you to reflect on how existential thought relates to your own experience of being in the world, to allow yourself to challenge your existing worldview and belief system, and to courageously explore potentially uncomfortable thoughts in order to build a more resilient framework for life, living and coaching. This is a process that takes time, and so each reader is encouraged to let these doors be opened, to digest and process what lies behind them, and to gradually integrate what you find useful into your existing coaching practice and the way you engage with work, life and the people around you.
- Not tell you exactly how existential coaching is done. Each coach will have to decide for themselves how best to let existential thought inform their practice. While there are common themes in existential practice, there is no single right way of doing it.
- Not try to convince you of anything or attempt to convert you to calling yourself an existential coach. I believe that any coach's practice will benefit from having spent some time reflecting on the "human condition", the many ways it affects people and how it shows up in the coaching room, regardless of your dominant approach to coaching or your specific process. Existential thinkers can add valuable insights on this topic. This book (ideally in combination with some dedicated training, coaching or other space where you find yourself in contact with other fellow human beings) will help you to strengthen or perhaps even develop your ability to encounter your clients in a more holistic way, taking into account all dimensions of their existence with an appreciation of the many challenges that life throws at each and every one of us, regardless of culture, gender, upbringing, socioeconomic background, health or other factors.

In the spirit of contracting, I feel it is important to mention that as human beings we tend to seek comfort, harmony and peace (the absence of inner conflict). As existential thinkers essentially uncover the inevitable inner conflict and dilemmas that sit at the core of the human experience, this book may confront you with some uncomfortable perspectives (some may go as far as to call them "truths", since they are certainly solid philosophical conclusions) about what it means to be human. Therefore it is important that you give yourself permission to keep reading with an awareness that some of the thoughts and ideas outlined in this book may clash with your existing worldview and may hence leave you with a feeling of uneasiness as you proceed to engage with the contents of this book. Throughout this book you will find reflective questions for you to consider that may lead you deep into an exploration of your own existence, who you are and how you relate with the world.

Personally I've made a decision to keep my eyes as open as possible and to explore as many of my blind spots as I can with regard to the world and myself in it, even if that means that I may have to face some of the darker sides of who I am, including irrational beliefs that keep me comfortable, areas where I avoid to face difficult decisions or situations in which I acted against what I believe in.

That said, I respect anybody who makes a conscious and deliberate choice not to know certain things for the sake of living more comfortably. Ignorance can be bliss. However, I decided that in the long run I live better when I dig as deep as possible into what (my) life is about and to understand as much as possible about the world. It is in the spirit of this quest for knowledge and understanding that I write, teach, coach, supervise, train, mentor, question and engage with my fellow human beings. It takes courage and it is certainly a challenging journey, but I have learned to embrace it and would not have it any other way. I'd be delighted if you joined me on this journey of exploration into what it means to be human and how we can use this understanding with our coaching clients.

Chapter 1

Coaching

What is coaching?

Coaching is a largely unregulated profession. While a number of private bodies[1] offer accreditation, guidelines for best practice and ethical frameworks, the term "Coach" is not protected and hence anybody may call themselves a coach and offer coaching services, whatever they may mean by this. Even in the academic literature on coaching, definitions vary considerably (Palmer & Whybrow, 2005) and are subject to much debate (Killburg, 1996; D'Abate et al., 2003). After more than a decade of additional research into coaching psychology (the scientific branch of psychology examining coaching practice and underlying theory) these statements still hold true. If you were to ask 100 coaches for their definition of what coaching is you are likely to get 100 different answers. And in a world where coaching services are being marketed to attract clients to often quite expensive packages, it is not surprising that practitioners try to carve out their own niche in an endeavour to promote their unique selling points and individual approach to practice. Yet even among coaching psychology researchers (who presumably pride themselves with objectivity and tend to stay clear from any agenda to further their own cause) definitions vary widely and range between "a form of tutoring or instruction" (Parsloe, 1995) to "just a different brand name for counselling work" (Carrol, 2003).

A very short history of coaching

While the origins of the profession have complex roots in sports, philosophy, psychology, mentoring, education and management, to notable development took place over the course of the last 50 years. In the 1970s tennis coach Timothy Gallwey proposed that beyond a certain level of skill, the players he coached fought their most challenging battles not against their opponents on the other side of the net but rather against their own mind. Subsequently he developed and published a system he called the Inner Game (Gallwey, 1972) and advocated that in order to learn and grow most effectively at high levels of athleticism the coach needed to create a space for the player to tune into his or her inner workings in order to perform at their best.

20 years later Sir John Whitmore introduced coaching into the workplace, and in his seminal work *Coaching for Performance* (published in 1992, with its fifth edition in 2017) put forward the most widely used process model for coaching practice, the GROW model. Rather than focusing on problems, pains and short-comings (as most therapeutic approaches adopt as a starting point), coaches start the process with the *goal* (G) in mind, and define it thoroughly before exploring where the client is now in relation to this goal – the *reality* (R). Once the discrepancy between where or who the client wants to be and where or who they are now is established, the coach facilitates the client's brainstorming of suitable *options* (O) to move towards their goal and subsequently create a clearly defined *way forward* (W), including an exploration of potential obstacles that may stand in the way of the client achieving the result. In order to boost effectiveness of the approach, goals and strategies were encouraged to be SMART (*specific, measurable, achievable, relevant* to personal values and beliefs, as well as *time-bound*). This proved to be a highly effective way to facilitate growth. Whitmore's definition of coaching is still one of the most widely used today: "Unlocking a person's potential to maximize their own performance. It is helping them to learn rather than teaching them."

The core elements of effective coaching

Looking at what contemporary conceptualisations of coaching have in common, van Nieuwerburgh (2017) identifies three key aspects and writes that coaching . . .

a) is a managed conversation that takes place between two people;
b) aims to support sustainable change to behaviours or ways of thinking; and
c) focuses on learning and development.

We may understand effective coaching practice to be composed of three elements (see Figure 1.1):

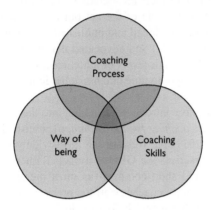

Figure 1.1 Coaching as conceptualised by van Nieuwerburgh (2017).

a)   the coach applying a specific process to manage the conversation and facilitate insights, learning and a way forward;

b)   utilising a set of key skills that assist this coaching process such as a.o. active listening, summarising, paraphrasing, asking powerful questions, reflecting back what is being heard, contracting (mutually agreeing on the framework, ground rules, direction, way of working etc.), bracketing assumptions, challenging; and

c)   adopting a specific way of being conducive to a strong coaching relationship that is signified by mutual trust and respect, empathy, congruence, positive regard, safety, openness, willingness to challenge and be challenged and to always hold the client's best interest as one's top priority.

Take a moment

Which of these three areas of coaching do you excel in? Which ones could you improve in and how? Are there other areas that you feel are important to good coaching practice? How would your own model or conceptualisation of the profession look like?

The crucial importance of the relationship – part I

While a coaching process can easily be adopted and skills can be learned, developing the "right" way of being can be more challenging as it is arguably a fuzzy concept and has not been explored in nearly enough depth as to make any substantiated claims as to what would be the most effective attitude toward meeting people that is likely to lead to the effective practice. What researchers, practitioners and clients tend to agree on is that the relationship between client and practitioner is the strongest predictor of success, regardless of how success may be defined by the client in the context of the coaching work (McKenna & Davis, 2009). Coaching is a meeting of two people with differing sets of values, worldviews and beliefs; and it is within this space that the client, through collaborative, open and honest dialogue with a fellow human being, may develop awareness and understanding of self in relation to others and their environment which ultimately leads to change, growth and transformation. And since every coach, as a human being, is unique in their way of being, then by this definition there are as many approaches to coaching as there are coaches. *"Who you are is how you coach"* is a maxim that has been ever present with me since my first mentor, Angela Jopling, passed down the message from her own mentor, and my student, supervisees and trainees seem to appreciate what the message entails: as long as you are authentically yourself and relate openly and honestly to another human being, curious about who and what you are being faced with and always focused on your client's ultimate agenda in an ethical way, you can practise whichever way you like and call it coaching as long as you contract clearly and transparently so that your client is able to provide informed consent to be coached by you.

And while coaching may not rely primarily on a relationship as described above, focusing more on skills and process (something that could soon be delivered by artificial intelligence) can provide a lot of value for clients, and it is widely accepted that it is the authentic human element that fuels the effectiveness of coaching.

Take a moment

To what extent are you paying attention to the relationship between you and your clients? Are you aware how it affects your coaching? Are you perhaps already practising humanistically? Are you discussing the nature of your relationships during your supervision? Or perhaps the relationship is less important to your particular approach to coaching (see e.g. Grant, 2014)?

The role of the coach

In each moment that we spend with a client we have to make choices as to how we interact with them. Depending on the practitioner's individual take on coaching in relation to what the client aims to achieve and always in the context of what mode of working has been mutually agreed on during the contracting phase, the role that the coach adopts in each moment or in general may vary. In an effort to distil the essence across the variety of roles that a coach may adopt during their interactions with clients (among others: sounding board, safe container, teacher, mentor, consultant, challenger, professional friend, fellow traveller, therapist, mirror or guru – see Jacob, 2013, and Sime & Jacob, 2018, for a review), a useful framework has been put forward by de Haan (2008). Typically the coach allows as much space as possible for the client to think, talk, feel and explore their situation, as this is where the majority of the solutions will be found. When the coach chooses to intervene (by speaking or otherwise), we have a variety of options across two main spectrums: exploring versus suggesting and supporting versus confronting or challenging (see Figure 1.2).

A good coach will move freely and appropriately across the whole spectrum of this playing field depending on what is likely to yield the best outcome for the client. This is where coaching reveals itself as a masterful art form due to the near infinite number of factors that would need to be considered on an ongoing basis in order to attempt to make the "right" decision as to how to interact with a client at any

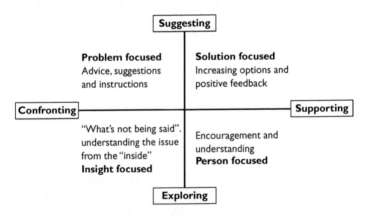

Figure 1.2 The playing field of a coach.

Source: based on de Haan (2008, p. 14)

given moment, in order to provide best service. There simply is no *one* right way of doing coaching and it often lies in the intuition of the coach informed by their training, experience and mindful presence that decisions are made, without any certainty with regards to whether the coach's decision was the best possible one to make. Attempting to cover the complexities of this process in full would go beyond the scope of this brief introduction. The reader without much knowledge of the foundation of coaching is hence referred to van Nieuwerburgh (2017), Whitmore (2017), de Haan (2008), Bird & Gornall (2016), Kline (2011) or Palmer & Whybrow (2007).

Take a moment

How do you see your role as a coach? What is your dominant or most natural style? How do you tend to respond to your clients?

A working definition of coaching

While there are plenty of definitions in circulation and a wide range of approaches has emerged as a result of individual differences on the part of the practitioner, the following working definition has been adopted as a starting point for exploring the existential approach:

> A conversation between the coach and coachee(s) in which the coach facilitates a journey of reflective discovery, decision-making and action, the defining characteristic of which is the focus on the coachee's own choices, solutions and agenda.
>
> (Bolton, 2017, p. 3)

Bolton adds:

> Of course, a statement like this may capture the basis of coaching but it doesn't capture the joy, excitement, challenge and reward. Nor does it capture the complexity of the process in terms of the feelings, thoughts, doubts, concerns, false turns and more on the part of the coach and client. However, as an overview of the defining character-istics of coaching it points to some key issues which remain consist-ent throughout most, if not all, coaching.
>
> (Bolton, 2017, p. 3)

Take a moment

What is your own definition of coaching? You may adapt one of the above (after a thorough challenge and spending some time reflecting on it in the context of your clients work, values and beliefs) or you may create your own.

What coaching is not

Given that nature of existential questions, it is important to at this point dedicate some space to an exploration of the boundaries of coaching practice and to underline the importance of ethics and reflective practice in an effort to safeguard clients. We shall return to the topic of ethics when we discuss the ethical dimension of existential coaching, yet it cannot be stressed enough that there are limits with regards to how far coaching (or rather you as a practitioner) can go so as not to cross the line to therapy (if you are not a trained therapist) or more generally to find yourself in a position where you are out of your depth and either feel or are unqualified to work with your client effectively, hence potentially putting your client, yourself or third parties at risk of psychological or even physical harm.

Consider therefore the following conceptualisations the differences between coaching and other approaches to helping-by-talking practices (Figures 1.3 and 1.4): de Haan's (2008) scope of coaching in the context of other forms of one-to-one learning and Fairley and Stout's (2004) map of talking practices across the two spectrum of asking questions versus giving answers and the practitioner's level of expertise on what their clients bring into the room.

The critically engaged reader will likely find at least a few aspects of the above conceptualisations that they would like to challenge and this is a sign that you have already put a lot of thought into the way that you see these professions, including their boundaries, commonalities and grey areas. Regardless of whether you agree with the specifics of such attempts to make sense of the landscape of one-to-one practices, an analysis of the available research, literature, surveys with practitioners and experiential accounts from clients, coaches and supervisors will show that coaching can reach quite far into other approaches but that the majority of it operates under the bell curve of largely performance, behaviour and solutions-focused interventions.

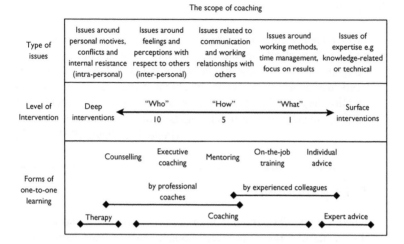

Figure 1.3 De Haan's (2008) understanding of the scope of coaching.

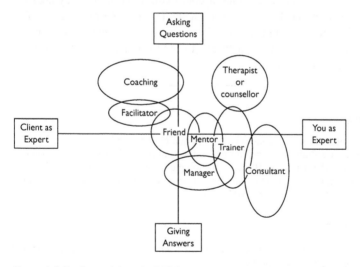

Figure 1.4 Fairley and Stout's (2004) illustration of the boundaries across various one-to-one professions.

The existential coach embraces a much larger spectrum of what may traditionally be seen as coaching practice and hence the lines can become blurry. Jopling (2008) writes about this *fuzzy space* and, in her work, explores differences and commonalities between psychotherapy and executive coaching. Popovic and Jinks illustrate this point well by pointing out that:

> within the coaching literature there appears to be an assumption that all coaching clients are mentally healthy, fully functioning and not inhibited by underlying psychological issues. Whilst coaching clients may appear to be robust and able to manage their emotions, in reality they could be just as vulnerable as counselling clients, but attempt to conceal their psychological problems (Maxwell, 2009).
>
> (Popovic & Jinks, 2013, p. 187)

Take a moment

Where do you draw the line between (your) coaching and other approaches of forms of practice? Looking back at your definition of coaching from above, where does it differ? What does it have in common? Is there a line or could you describe the grey area? At what point do you refer a client? Try to write down a set of guidelines for yourself as to when you are overstepping your competencies or realm of practice and what to do in these situations to ensure ethical practice.

Note

1 Among the largest ones are the International Coaching Federation (ICF), the Association for Coaching (AC), the European Mentoring and Coaching Council (EMCC), the British Psychological Society's (BPS) Special Group in Coaching Psychology and the Association for Professional Executive Coaching and Supervision (APECS).

References

Bird, J., & Gornall, S. (2016). *The Art of Coaching: A Handbook of Tips and Tools*. New York: Routledge.

Bolton, N. (2017). *Foundations*. Unpublished manuscript. London: Animas Centre for Coaching.

Carroll, M. (2003). The new kid on the block. *Counselling Psychology Journal, 14*(10), 28–31.

D'Abate, C.P., Eddy, E.R., & Tannenbaum, S.I. (2003). What's in a name? A literature-based approach to understanding mentoring, coaching, and other constructs that describe developmental interactions. *Human Resource Development Review, 2*(4), 360–384.

De Haan, E. (2008). *Relational Coaching: Journeys towards Mastering One-to-One Learning.* Chichester, UK: Wiley.

Fairley, S.G., & Stout, C.E. (2004). *Getting Started in Personal and Executive Coaching.* Hoboken, NJ: John Wiley & Sons.

Gallwey, T. (1972). *The Inner Game of Tennis.* London: Bantam Books.

Grant, A. (2014). Autonomy support, relationship satisfaction and goal focus in the coach–coachee relationship: which best predicts coaching success? *Coaching: An International Journal of Theory, Research and Practice, 7*(1), 18–38.

Jacob, Y.U. (2013). Exploring boundaries of existential coaching. Master's thesis. Retrieved from www.academia.edu/8376861/Exploring_Boundaries_of_Existential_Coaching

Joplin, A. (2008). The fuzzy space: exploring the experience of the space between psychotherapy and executive coaching. Unpublished MSc dissertation, New School of Psychotherapy and Counselling, London, UK. Retrieved from http://de.scribd.com/doc/17168879/Research-Thesis-The-Fuzzy-Space-Between-Psychotherapy-and-Executive-Coaching

Kilburg, R.R. (1996). Toward a conceptual understanding and definition of executive coaching. *Consulting Psychology Journal: Practice and Research, 48*(2), 59–60.

Kline, N. (2011). *Time to Think: Listening to Ignite the Human Mind.* London: Octopus Publishing Book.

Maxwell, A. (2009). How do business coaches experience the boundary between coaching and therapy/counselling? *Coaching: An International Journal of Theory, Research and Practice, 2*(2), 149–162.

McKenna, D., & Davis, S.L. (2009). Hidden in plain sight: the Active Ingredients of Executive Coaching. *Industrial and Organizational Psychology, 2,* 244–260.

Palmer, S., & Whybrow, A. (2005). The proposal to establish a special group in coaching psychology. *The Coaching Psychologist, 1,* 5–12.

Palmer, S., & Whybrow, A. (2007). *Handbook of Coaching Psychology.* Hove, UK: Routledge.

Parsloe, E. (1995). *Coaching, Mentoring and Assessing: A Practical Guide in Developing Competence.* London: Nichols Publishing.

Popovic, N., & Jinks, D. (2013). *Personal Consultancy.* London: Routledge.

Sime, C., & Jacob, Y.U. (2018). Crossing the line? A qualitative exploration of ICF master certified coaches' perception of roles, borders and boundaries. *International Coaching Psychology Review, 13*(2), 46–61.

Van Nieuwerburgh, C. (2017). *An Introduction to Coaching Skills: A Practical Guide* (2nd edition). London: Sage.

Whitmore, J. (1992). *Coaching for Performance.* London: Nicholas Brealey.

Whitmore, J. (2017). *Coaching for Performance* (5th edition). London: Nicholas Brealey.

Chapter 2

Existential coaching

Existential coaching is an approach that is rooted in and informed by existential philosophy, a branch of philosophy concerned with questions of existence – that is, what it means to exist, to be human and to be alive in a world with other people (more on this in the next section).

It has developed out of the practical application of these philosophical ideas (more on these in Chapter 4) and is hence indebted to a range of practices such as philosophical consultancy (Achenbach, 1984, 2002; Hoogendijk, 1988), personal existential analysis (Längle, 1993, 1999; Batthyány, 2016), existential counselling and psychotherapy (Cooper, 2003; van Deurzen, 1999; Yalom, 1980), as well as those coaching approaches that strayed away from the traditional performance and behaviour focus as to include in-depth conversations about the nature and experience of being (e.g. ontological coaching; see Sieler, 2011).

Since the early 2000s, pioneers such as Emmy van Deurzen, Monica Hanaway, Ernesto Spinelli, Bruce Peltier, Caroline Horner, Alfried Längle, Mike van Oudtshoorn, Jamie Reed and others started to integrate principles and practices from existential philosophy and phenomenology into their work with clients and organisations. However, training opportunities for existentially informed coaching only emerged fairly recently[1] and the only full-length book publications to date are *Existential Perspectives on Coaching* (van Deurzen & Hanaway, 2012), *Existential Coaching Skills: The Handbook* (Hanaway & Reed, 2014; Hanaway, 2018) and a German-language book, *Existentielles Coaching* (Längle & Bürgi, 2014).

Practical existential philosophy is about human lived experience and as such the existential coach has typically not only explored these questions theoretically and philosophically, but will have made their own experiences with the inevitable struggles and challenges that living brings with it. The existentially minded coach is eager to live a full life and does not shy away from courageously facing life's many challenges. With this understanding, on a philosophical and practical level, the existential coach is able to identify existential concerns in a client's narrative.

Since most of our actions, behaviours and motivations are influenced at a fundamental level by these existential concerns, reflecting them back to the client will foster an understanding of the self at a deep level and open up new possibilities for choice, to help clients assume ultimate freedom and responsibility with regard to their existence.

Existential coaching is a place to think, ponder, reflect and explore the human condition in the context of a specific goal. It helps clients to identify areas of self-deception (blind spots), to create more opportunity and choice, and to live a more authentic and full life in spite of (and indeed because of) inevitable existential anxiety (German: *Angst*) that accompanies living in this world with other people.

To illustrate the value of this angst, consider Leijssen (2014), who describes it as "wake-up calls for realizing the full potential of human life". What the existential approach to coaching can add to your practice is an acknowledgement of the darker sides of life (tackling negatives, difficulties and anxieties) and the ability to help clients face these things with courage and responsibility, enabling them to take action and assume their ultimate freedom so that they can live the way they want to live.

Therefore, we can broadly adopt a definition of existential coaching as "an approach with an entirely pragmatic objective: to help people to live their lives with greater deliberation, liberty, understanding and passion" (van Deurzen & Hanaway, 2012, p. xvi).

Take a moment

When you think about the word "existence" as it relates to existential coaching what comes up for you?

Existentialism in a nutshell

Existentialism is a branch of philosophy that falls under the umbrella of humanism. It is concerned with the fundamental questions of what it means to exist and how people experience "being" (or being there, German: *Dasein*). Hence, it is a philosophy of human lived experience. Since we cannot observe or measure "being", existential thinkers use philosophy to gain knowledge and insight about some of the foundational questions about human existence as to get closer to the core of this experience.

Consider this thought experiment. When we strip away everything that defines us as human beings in this world (our jobs, the people we know, the colour of our skin, our personal characteristics, and anything that is not concerned with mere existence), we can start to think about what it means and how it feels just to be (as compared to being *something*). If we strip away everything that we think we are, all the things we have, all the characteristics we inherited or developed, the activities we do and the skills we have learnt, even the language we speak and what makes up our identity, then we arrive at the bare backbones of existence.

Take a moment

In an attempt to get closer to the feeling described above, complete the sentence "I am . . ." as many ways as you can. You might write things like: "I am intelligent", "I am tired", "I am Scottish", "I am a mother", "I am funny".[2] Afterwards, gradually imagine yourself without these attributes, things, relationships or whatever you listed above. Go on a journey to imagine stripping these away one by one. How does it feel as you start to lose these labels?[3] This is the process of disidentification which invites us to lose the labels that we so often allow to define us and limit how we show up in the world.

The philosophical study of being is called ontology and as such is concerned with questions about the nature of reality, existence, becoming and our relationship with the world. Philosophy is a method of inquiry in order to create knowledge about aspect that neither be measured nor observed. Philosophers use logic and reason in order to arrive at conclusions about the metaphysical and can hence contribute valuable insights to areas in which science or common sense are at their wit's end.

Using philosophy, existential thinkers concluded that we can only really know two things about existence at the very foundation: that we *are* (alive, existing, as compared to non-being) and that there are other people in this world. In other words, being is never a disembodied, non-relational experience. *Living with others* is a given of our existence – something we cannot change.

If we are alive, we cannot avoid being in the world with others. Even when others are not visible or currently around us, it is inevitable that we are born of other people and relate to them in some way or another. We also have no control over where or when we are born, something Heidegger referred to as our "throwness", or as our being "thrown" into this world.

The concept of givens relates to the unavoidable realities of human existence. There are a number of givens that we will explore in the course of this book which are particularly relevant to existential coaching, the main ones being temporality (our existence within time), mortality (death), uncertainty, meaning-making, isolation, freedom/choice/responsibility and authenticity. Collectively, these are often referred to as "the human condition" – that is, the consequences of merely being alive and existing in the world with, or in relation to, other people.

Take a moment

I invite you to pause for a few minutes and think about the human condition, your existence. What do you experience that is an unavoidably part of being human? What are the givens and how do they show up? What is it like to be in the world for you? What can we not change as a result of being alive and here with others? Write down as many givens as you can?

As a result of this "human condition" and the givens of human existence, existential philosophers have concluded that all of us experience what they called existential anxiety, a form of anxiety that goes beyond normal anxiety in that it is a result of being alive in this world with others, and in that it won't go away – at least, not if we aim to live consciously and authentically. I added this last part because there is in fact a way to live without this anxiety, at least temporarily: we can deny this anxiety by deceiving ourselves, by closing our eyes to some of the realities of our existence (for example that we might die tomorrow).

However, if we are to live a full life, the existentialist will argue that we need to face the uncomfortable existential givens and courageously interact with the world in spite of its many challenges and the anxiety that goes with it. The reward is living courageously with open eyes, embracing life's challenges and uncertainties as the *stuff* that makes life exciting and, indeed, worth living. We will explore this in more depth when we talk about each existential theme in more detail.

The first person who wrote about the human condition in this way was the Danish philosopher Søren Kierkegaard. Other major thinkers were Friedrich Nietzsche, Martin Heidegger and Martin Buber in Germany; Jean Paul Sartre, Simone de Beauvoir, Maurice Merleau-Ponty and Albert Camus in France; and Rollo May, Irvin Yalom and Paul Tillich in the US. Most of existentialism's main thinkers are from the Western hemisphere, in part because of its relative affluence creating more time for its people to think and philosophise.

An overview of existential thinkers as well as practitioners can be found in Tables 2.1 and 2.2 (as depicted by leading British existential psychotherapist and coach Emmy van Deurzen). If you would like to immerse yourself in existential philosophy and practice, I recommend looking into these authors in more depth. It takes a little while to process and grasp existential philosophy and the more you read, reflect upon these ideas and connect them to your own life experiences, the more you will benefit.

One of the main tenets of existential thought is that, when it comes to the experience of being, there is no single Truth (with a capital T – meaning overarching and objective). What we experience is subjective and every human being will construct their own worldview (meanings, values and beliefs). As a result, we are all unique, which fundamentally puts us in conflict with each other. There are a number of other polarities, inner conflicts and contradictions that we will inevitably be confronted with in the course of our lifetime. Existential practitioners argue that only to the extent in which we learn to accept and live with these can we succeed in living a full life (meaning experiencing the whole spectrum of what it has to offer us).

The issue in this day and age is that many people become increasingly alienated (German: *entfremdet*) from what it actually means to be. Technology and consumerism have led us to believe that it is possible to live comfortably on a continuous basis. Therefore, once we encounter a "boundary situation" (a confrontation with one of the existential givens/ dilemmas) and experience existential anxiety, we try to make this feeling go away, rather than using it as an opportunity to learn, to explore and live life, or to grow and better understand life. Instead of living courageously, with resoluteness (German: *Entschlossenheit*, which can literally be translated as "de-closed-ness"), we long for release/letting be (German: *Gelassenheit*).

Table 2.1 Existential philosophers

Philosophers of freedom	Phenomenologists	Existentialists	Post-structuralists	Existential-humanists
Søren Kierkegaard 1813–1855	Franz Brentano 1838–1917	Jean-Paul Sartre 1905–1980	Michel Foucault 1926–1984	Martin Buber 1878–1965
Friedrich Nietzsche 1844–1900	Edmund Husserl 1859–1938	Maurice Merleau-Ponty 1908–1961	Emmanuel Levinas 1905–1995	Paul Tillich 1886–1965
Arthur Schopenhauer 1788–1860	Karl Jaspers 1883–1969	Simone de Beauvoir 1908–1986	Paul Ricoeur 1913–2005	Rollo May 1909–1994
Fyodor Dostoyevski 1821–1881	Martin Heidegger 1889–1976	Gabriel Marcel 1889–1973	Jacques Lacan 1901–1981	Hannah Arendt 1906–1975
Karl Marx 1818–1883	Max Scheler 1874–1928	Albert Camus 1913–1960	Jacques Derrida 1930–2004	Abraham Maslow 1908–1970

Source: van Deurzen (2015)

Table 2.2 Existential practitioners

Early psychiatrists	Humanistic psychologists	British alternative	Recent Americans	Recent British
Ludwig Binswanger 1881–1966	Paul Tillich 1886–1965	George Kelly 1905–1967	James Bugental 1915–2008	Hans Cohn 1916–2004
Karl Jaspers 1883–1969	Carl Rogers 1902–1987	Aaron Esterson 1923–1999	Thomas Szasz 1920–	Freddie Strasser 1924–2008
Eugene Minkowski 1885–1972	Rollo May 1909–1994	Ronald Laing 1927–1989	Irvin Yalom 1931–	Ernesto Spinelli 1949–
Medard Boss 1904–1990	Viktor Frankl 1905–1997	David Cooper 1931–1986	Kirk Schneider 1956–	Emmy van Deurzen 1951–

Source: van Deurzen (2015)

Following existential thought, it is impossible to live anxiety-free, comfortable or happy for any prolonged period of time except at times when we are distracted or so engaged with something that we simply do not have the headspace to think about it. These states, however, cannot last and sooner or later we will inevitable be brought face to face with our human condition. The existential "solution" is to learn to embrace a life that will give us lemons – as these lemons are what makes life exciting and worth living. For example, without the experience of sadness, we would not know what it is like to be happy. Human beings can and do adapt to almost any circumstances, pleasant as well as uncomfortable (with the exception of occurrences such as random loud noise or the loss of a child). Hence, if we were continuously happy, we would experience happiness as our normal state of being and therefore would need to experience higher degrees of happiness in order to feel good, while feeling only a small amount of happiness would be perceived as the new "sad". We live in comparison to what we are used to, a blessing when times are challenging and a curse when times are good but static, hence our tendency to suffer in times of prosperity as we crave change.

Existential philosophy has a lot to offer for those who aim to live their lives in full, prepared to embrace both the desirable positives and the often avoided (and misleadingly called) "negatives" of human existence. The existential view is that the whole spectrum of human experience is precious, valuable and meaningful, and that, without the existential givens, life would indeed be dull, boring and predictable.

Take a moment

Think about your life. Is there anything that you have been consistently trying to avoid, such as getting hurt, feeling sad, or disappointment? To what extent have you been successful? Which ones are worth fighting against and which are perhaps better accepted?

How does existential coaching differ from other coaching approaches?

As noted earlier, existential coaches are interested in, and inspired by, the big questions of life. Therefore, quite naturally, existential coaching is a lot closer to the counselling realm than other approaches to coaching, and may indeed at times operate close to the boundary of therapy, if not past that boundary. This notion obviously depends on where you define this boundary to be – something that is still an ongoing debate among practitioners in both vocations. For a more detailed discussion see Popovic and Jinks (2013) or Jacob (2013).

Some of the big questions

- How should I live?
- Where do I want to go? What do I want to do with my life?
- Who am I?
- What does it mean to be (alive)?
- Why am I in this world? What is the meaning/value/purpose of my existence?
- What can and can't I change?
- How can I be happy?
- How do I make the right choices?
- What is expected of me?
- What should I do with my life?
- Where do I belong?
- How should I act and be in relation to other people?
- Is there fairness in the world? How can I make sense of pain and suffering?
- Can I make a change for the better and to what extent is change possible?
- Is it possible to understand life and get a grip on it?
- Can I find ways of overcoming my troubles?
- Is it necessary to suffer this much?
- How can I live a life that's worthwhile?

Take a moment

Let the above questions sink in. What are some of your own big questions?

It is important to note that clients will not often bring these big questions into coaching to start with. However, when a client has an important issue or a challenge, it is likely that, on some level, at least some of these big questions profoundly influence their thinking, feelings and behaviours.

For example, a client may approach you for time management issues, and wanting to exercise more in order to feel more energised. In the process of the coaching, they then identify that the main obstacle in the way of reaching this goal is working a job that is not meaningful to them and that drains them of most of their energy on a daily basis. Also, due to a recent event, they have found themselves thinking about changing careers; this thought has been on their mind, making it difficult to concentrate and do their work. At this point, with this understanding in mind, the client needs to make a decision as to whether they want to continue with a behavioural approach, in order to change their behaviour (exercise more and work more productively), or to whether they want to tackle the underlying source of their issue (planning to change jobs). An exploration informed by an existential lens opens up possibilities for the client that may be invaluable.

Take a moment

How does the existential approach to coaching differ from your current approach to coaching? What could an understanding of existential philosophy add to your practice?

Existential concerns are often at the heart of important decisions. It can be useful to bring these concerns into awareness, or at least to have a sense of the client's worldview – which then opens up an understanding of them as a whole person existing in this world.

This also means that ethics are of special importance to coaches who practise existentially. This is because we need to negotiate with ourselves to what extent we are able to work with somebody in a coaching context and, sometimes, when it would be better for the client to see a therapist. I encourage all practitioners to keep this question in mind and to explore their understanding of where this boundary might be in their understanding of coaching.

Take a moment

Assume for a moment that your client brings one of the big questions into the coaching space and has identified a struggle to find meaning in their life as an obstacle to their goal. To what extent

(continued)

(continued)

do you feel you are able to work with that client, and at what point would it be best for all stakeholders for this client to be referred to a therapist? Consider your previous training, the contract you have with the client, how you introduced your practice, the code of ethics of any professional body you belong to, and the law – as well as your own comfort zone.

Existential coaches are more likely to be open to talking about deeply emotional subjects, challenging experiences and things that are potentially upsetting. Helping a client to open their eyes to some of life's dilemmas and its inevitable challenges – so that they may develop the ability to live courageously – can be a precarious journey. It is of utmost importance to take all measures to keep your client safe and allow them to make an informed decision on whether or not to work with you.

Another difference is that many coaching approaches focus solely on the positives – on strengths or on specific themes, such as time management, mindfulness, relationships, increasing performance or changing habits. The existential approach tries to grasp the person as a whole and to help them better understand themselves and their worldview, thus building a solid foundation on which difficult decisions can be made.

Clients will learn to embrace all aspects of living life – the positives as well as the negatives – and in the process learn to accept the givens of existence. As a result, they will be more conscious in their everyday life and better able to accept the inevitable struggles of living in this day and age.

Existential coaching's main differences from more popular coaching approaches are its roots in philosophy and its openness to exploring the big questions of existence (see below) in a coaching context. Another important element is the fact that there is no unified school of existentialism. Since existential thinking encourages people to challenge dogma and to explore and construct one's own knowledge and worldview, there is no accepted thought leader in the field. Each existential thinker builds her or his own framework based on their own subjective experiences and upbringing, and hence constructs their own individual worldview and understanding of existential thought. What all of us have in common is an acknowledgement of the existential givens at a fundamental level.

Take a moment

At the beginning of a session, during the initial contracting stage, how would you introduce existential coaching or the fact that you may include elements of existential coaching in your practice?

Who uses it, why and when?

In this section I would like to differentiate between existential coaches (those who specialise in openly discussing existential life issues, big questions and personal dilemmas in a coaching context) and coaches whose practice is *informed* by existential philosophy but who may not choose to work specifically on existential topics. It is useful for the coach to have an understanding of what it means to be alive in this world, and for the client it may be immensely valuable to identify any relation that a situation might have with underlying existential concerns (given that these can act as obstacles to growth with regard to the client's goal).

The target group for people who will at some point be confronted with existential questions, concerns and anxiety, and therefore are likely to benefit from existential coaching, is people in the world with other people. As such, existential coaching will be valuable to anyone who is open to exploring these issues courageously and not afraid to talk about things that may be deeply personal.

Many of our feelings, behaviours and thoughts (especially particularly challenging ones) are related to our existential concerns, even if these may not be brought openly into the coaching space. For example, a client might talk about procrastination and motivation, and in the course of the coaching you may identify the underlying issue that this is connected to.

Clients may approach you at a time of crisis as an alternative to therapy or counselling, because many people still think that therapy is only for people who are mentally ill, while they themselves feel well, able to think clearly, and able to cope appropriately with daily life. As such, they wish to avoid the stigma that may accompany traditional helping-by-talking approaches. In my existential coaching training, we termed this phenomenon "therapy through the back door" (Jacob, 2011).

Existential coaching may also be used to build defences – that is, resilience against future challenges. Clients may learn to embrace existential anxiety (as compared to the normal kind of anxiety that can be cured or alleviated). The coaching process will help the client to understand what they can change and what they need to accept as a given (what they can't change), along with, most importantly, how to tell the difference between the two with regard to their goals and aspirations.

Clients may also simply have a longing for a place to ponder, reflect, think and understand life better – a place that is free from the stigma of therapy and where they are not told what to do or how to live, while still being challenged openly and respectfully on their assumptions. That way they are able to get to know themselves better and strengthen their foundation of character, which enables them to make difficult decisions in the future from an authentic sense of self.

Take a moment

Think about the sort of clients you would like to work with and the goals they would want to work on. In what way can the existential approach to coaching add value?

Who are your clients?

If you plan to work within an existential coaching framework, it is helpful to consider who your potential clients are and to consider what kind of person may benefit most from utilising an existential approach to coaching. People naturally desire quick-fix solutions – metaphorical or literal magic pills – and many coaching approaches happily provide answers and share experience. This means that an existential approach to one-to-one work will not be the preferred choice for every client. It works best for someone who . . .

- Is willing to engage in the process of exploring and re-evaluating their assumptions, beliefs and worldview.
- Wishes to develop a certain level of self awareness and understanding.
- Is willing and courageous enough to face and explore the unknown.
- Values the following basic assumptions about human nature (as derived by van Deurzen & Adams, 2011, p. 41):

o   It is possible to make sense of life.
o   It is good to do so.
o   Each person has the capacity for making informed decisions about their life and their attitude towards it.
o   Difficult issues will not be resolved by being avoided.
o   Human nature is basically flexible.
o   People are able to learn from life and transcend problems.

As van Deurzen (1997, p. 200) summarises: "If there is no readiness to enter a philosophical exploration of their personal world it is unlikely that much existential work can be accomplished."

Take a moment

How would you know that your client is ready to enter a philosophical exploration of their personal world? How could you invite them in a way that is ethical and transparent? Are there other ways in which may help clients be interested in these questions? How can we create this space?

Mindset and attitude of an existential coach

Working from an existential perspective requires a certain set of attitudes and skills that can and need to be developed in order to deliver good and ethical practice (see van Deurzen & Adams, 2011). Existential practitioners . . .

- Will have a certain degree of training, including aspects of psychotherapy.
- Will have, to some degree, grappled with existential issues and developed an awareness of and an ability to identify existential themes when they present themselves.
- Regard the client as fundamentally equal, and their own role to be that of fellow traveller, rather than an expert.
- Value their own assumptions and beliefs but are willing and able to bracket them during phenomenological exploration of the client's experience.

- Do not shy away from challenging or speaking openly and directly about their doubts, curiosities or opinions when relevant to the client's agenda.
- Are willing and motivated to make sense of their own lives; are constantly aware of, evaluating and re-evaluating their assumptions, beliefs and past experiences; and cherish and utilise their capacity for learning, growth and change. They accept that their own worldview is, at best, temporarily coherent and are therefore open to being challenged and engaging in constant exploration of life's paradoxes and difficulties.

I recognize myself when my value system becomes too tidy and my life too neatly organized and my views too secure and my whole being too self-righteously existential. Then it is time to let myself be plunged back into the abyss of life, from where I have to rediscover what attracted me to this way of working in the first place. [. . .] Those who sound too self-assured and too definite about what makes a [practitioner] existential, or those who are too sure that existential is right, are clearly out of touch with forces that determine matters of life or death.

(van Deurzen, 1997, pp. 200–201)

You can see that working existentially as well as sitting on the receiving end of existential work may not be suitable for every client or indeed coach. It requires a belief in a set of assumptions about the world and people and requires a higher degree of courage and willingness to engage in challenging conversation and exploration than many other approaches to coaching. If you are planning to become an existential coach it is important that you reflect carefully, on yourself, your beliefs around coaching, your broader worldview and your ability and willingness to practise at this level of depth and complexity. If your endeavour is to let existential thought inform your existing practice then the above can be taken somewhat more lightly.

Notes

1   The iCoaching Academy started to offer coach training with existential underpinnings in the early 2000s. The first Master's programme (MA Existential Coaching) was established in 2010 in London. Further existential coaching training opportunities are listed in the references and resources towards the end of this book.
2   In a recent workshop attendees struggled to strip away their sense of humour ("I am funny"). Imagine that you move to a different culture in which people

just don't get your sense of humour so that gradually you stop regarding yourself as funny also.

3 If you write down "I am alive", then you found the one attribute that will be very difficult to strip away mentally. It also defies the point of the exercise because if we're not being alive, we don't exist (at least form an existential perspective) and hence it won't be possible to get any closer towards experiencing what mere existence may feel like.

References

Achenbach, G.B. (1984). *Philosophische Praxis*. Köln: Verlag für Philosophie Jürgen Dinter.

Achenbach, G.B. (2002). Philosophical Practice opens up the trace to Lebenskönnerschaft. In H. Herrestad, A. Holt and H. Svare (eds), *Philosophy in Society*. Oslo: Unipub Forlag.

Batthyány, A. (2016). *Logotherapy and Existential Analysis: Proceedings of the Viktor Frankl Institute Vienna*. Cham, Switzerland: Springer.

Cooper, M. (2003). *Existential Therapies*. Thousand Oaks, CA: Sage.

Hanaway, M. (2018). *Existential Coaching Skills: The Handbook* (2nd edition). Guernsey: Corporate Harmony.

Hanaway, M., & Reed, J. (2014). *Existential Coaching Skills: the Handbook*. Corporate Harmony.

Hoogendijk, A. (1988). *Spreekuur bij een filosoof*. Utrecht: Veers.

Jacob, Y.U. (2011). Therapy through the back-door: the call for integrative approaches to one-to-one talking practices and existential coaching as a possible framework. Unpublished manuscript. Retrieved from www.coachingandmediation.net/downloads/01%20-%20Research%20&%20Publications/2011-Jacob-Therapy_Through_the_Back_Door.pdf

Jacob, Y.U. (2013). Exploring boundaries of existential coaching. Master's thesis. Retrieved from www.academia.edu/8376861/Exploring_Boundaries_of_Existential_Coaching

Längle, A. (1993). A practical application of Personal Existential Analysis (PEA) – a therapeutic conversation for finding oneself. Retrieved from www.scribd.com/document/367937679/A-practical-application-of-Personal-Existential-Analysis-pdf

Längle, A. (1999). The Process of Diagnosis in Existential Analysis. In H. Bartuska, M. Buchsbaumer, G. Mehta, G. Pawlowsky & S. Wiesnagrotzki (eds), *Psychotherapeutic Diagnosis. Guidelines for the New Standard* (pp. 83–90). New York: Springer.

Längle, A., & Bürgi, D. (2014). *Existentielles Coaching: Theoretische Orientierung, Grundlagen und Praxis für Coaching, Organisationsberatung und Supervision*. Vienna: Facultas Universitäsverlag.

Leijssen, M. (2014). Existential wellbeing counselling. In G. Madison (ed.), *Emerging Practice in Focusing-Oriented Psychotherapy. Innovative Theory, Applications and Practice* (pp. 142–157). London: Jessica Kingsley Publishers.

Popovic, N., & Jinks, D. (2013). *Personal Consultancy*. London: Routledge.

Sieler, A. (2011). Ontological coaching. In E. Cox, T. Bachkirova & D. Clutterbuck (eds), *The Complete Handbook of Coaching* (pp. 107–119). London: Sage.

van Deurzen, E. (1997). *Everyday Mysteries*. London: Routledge.

van Deurzen, E. (1999). Existentialism and existential psychotherapy. In C. Mace (ed.), *Heart and Soul: The Therapeutic Face of Philosophy* (pp. 216–235). Florence, KY: Taylor & Frances/Routledge.

van Deurzen, E., & Adams, M. (2011). *Skills in Existential Counselling and Psychotherapy*. London: Sage.

van Deurzen, E., & Hanaway, M. (2012). *Existential Perspectives on Coaching*. Basingtoke, UK: Palgrave Macmillan.

Yalom, I.D. (1980). *Existential Psychotherapy*. New York: Basic Books.

Chapter 3

Existentialism

The human condition and our quest for happiness

Above, we introduced the givens of existence and the human condition. It is useful to break existence down to this level because it helps us understand what all people have in common at a fundamental level. And while all the great existential thinkers (and often do-ers) have disagreed on a whole range of issues, they all agree that being human involves experiencing anxiety. This is inevitable. We cannot be free from anxiety. Yet so many people seek comfort and happiness beyond what we could realistically expect from life.

Product advertising as well as the way people advertise themselves (for jobs or on platforms such as Facebook, LinkedIn, etc.) portray an often unattainable ideal of a human being (Nietzsche's "*Übermensch*", or superman). Existentialists, coaches, psychologists, therapists and pretty much everybody who has been in open, honest and direct psychological contact with another human being will pretty much guarantee you that all human beings experience anxiety and inner conflicts throughout their lives. Some more and some less, but nobody can live anxiety-free for long periods of time. If somebody tells you that they have freed themselves from all anxiety then they are either lying, they have deluded themselves successfully (by suppressing memories of feeling anxious), they keep themselves constantly engaged, busy or distracted as to not allow any time to be still and tune in to their feelings (and hence are on a sure-fire way towards burnout[1]) or there is something seriously wrong with their brain chemistry. Again, it is important to highlight the difference between existential anxiety (caused by an awareness of confrontation with the givens of existence – inevitable) and other forms of anxiety (such as getting anxious ahead of a public speaking gig, which can be alleviated or even eliminated through preparations, experience, a shift in mindset or other techniques).

While *sitting with* and exploring an uncomfortable emotion such as anxiety can be of great value (our emotions are a great opportunity to learn and often act as a compass for finding aspects of our life that matter so much to us that they make us feel something), it is not surprising that many people would want to lessen or altogether avoid these "negative" feelings. It is a natural human instinct to avoid pain and suffering and thrive towards happiness. And this process often happens fast and below the level of our conscious awareness. The existentialist, in an attempt to live consciously aware of their inner workings and live their lives as fully aware as possible, will not shy away from these uncomfortable feelings but rather move forward with their life *despite* these feelings (German: *trotzdem*) in the knowledge that they are an important teacher as well as completing their human experience and allowing them to go through life with open eyes.

Idle talk, bad faith and existential resilience

People tend to avoid getting in contact with the existential spectrum. Heidegger (1962) conceptualised "idle talk" (German: *Gerede*) as using language and talking to people without saying much of real meaning or value in relation to their experience of being in the world. We talk for the sake of keeping our minds off an awareness of our human condition. Similarly, Sartre (1958) talked about a phenomenon he coined *bad faith* (French: *mauvaise foi*), which is the unconscious process of denying one's freedom to choose (which as a pleasant side-effect allows us to reject responsibility for our life situation or not taking meaningful action to induce positive, yet difficult to achieve changes in our life). Frequently, in my coaching room as well as "out there" in the world, I see and hear people making excuses for why they are not pursuing this or that course of action (reaching from the mundane to the life-changing), often in an attempt not to face the uncertainty of chartering into the unknown and making themselves uncomfortable in the process. And regularly I catch myself doing the same thing. It is, after all, only human to try and avoid suffering.

While it seems that many became very good at suppressing existential anxiety, denying it, drinking it away or pushing it out of their awareness in some other way, it is undeniable that this is ultimately not a healthy process, or at the very least won't allow a client to move forward and live to their full potential. It may be a good defence mechanism in the short term in times when we need to stay focused and functional (for example during a time of crisis). However, suppressed anxiety (whether this is a conscious or unconscious process) always comes back in some form or another and the longer we avoid it, the harder it will hit us when it re-emerges, at times in the form of symptoms seemingly unrelated to its original cause (such as a belly ache or back pain that a doctor is unable to link to a physiological cause). At that point it is often difficult to untangle the underlying web of inner workings that led to these symptoms and the only solution at this stage may be lengthy psychotherapy in order to explore the now-obscured web of relations in depth. Existential coaching invites clients to face their human condition and the challenges of their existence at the time that they emerge. This requires ongoing courageous engagement but will ultimately lead to a clearer picture of the self in relation to one's environment and likely shield us from times of (severe) crisis in the future, something I call "existential resilience".

The goal here, I should add, may not be an ever-present awareness of one's potentially imminent death or the uncertainty of everything, to attempt to have meaningful and deep conversation at all times or to constantly tune in to your underlying existential anxiety. This may in fact be what drove many existential thinkers and writers into long periods of depression or even madness in some cases. The invitation is to take time regularly to reflect on your life situation and choices in relation to your values, beliefs and what is important to you at a deeper level as to check that you are not avoiding doing the right thing (by your own standards) in an attempt to live comfortably, or, if you do choose to live comfortably, to do so in conscious awareness of the consequences of the growing incongruence and feelings of inauthenticity that accompany such choices (keep in mind that even those who define their life philosophy as purely hedonistic and hence pursue to live as enjoyable a life as possible, often suffer as they get to an age where this may be challenging to uphold or they begin to crave a deeper meaning in their existence).

Take a moment

Living in denial can have positive and negative effects on your life. Take a moment to think about a situation in which you have strongly believed in something that turned out not to be true, but that has helped you in some way (for example, this could be a

(continued)

(continued)

belief that you could win a race against tough competition and, as a result, you trained extra hard and ended up in a respectable ninth place rather than not even signing up).

Afterwards, think of a time when you ended up in a predicament because you did not allow yourself to see the likely implications of a certain course of action or did not pursue a course of action in order to stay comfortable and safe (for example speaking to somebody you were attracted to at an event or pitching your business idea to an investor).

Can you think of an example like this from your coaching? How could you help a client become more aware of their choices and alternative possibilities? Is it worth inducing some discomfort for your client by helping them to be more aware of their choices and to challenge their excuses? How can you do this ethically?

The four dimensions of existence, the paradoxes of life and key themes in existentialism

All human beings experience dilemmas, paradoxes and inner conflicts on several levels or dimensions: the physical (German: *Umwelt*, or environment), the social (*Mitwelt*, or "with-world", the personal (*Eigenwelt*, or "own-world") and the spiritual (*Überwelt*, or super/over-world). Based on Binswanger (1963), Yalom (1980) and van Deurzen-Smith (1984), these dimensions are described well and in more detail in Cooper (2003), and also very tangibly in van Deurzen and Hanaway (2012). The key themes and paradoxes in existential thought operate on these four dimensions, and therefore it is useful to structure this section in four parts, accordingly.

Physical dimension – temporality and death

Take a moment

Bard Canning (2007) opened an essay on death with the following words: "Surely death is the greatest threat that we all face. For many people, it gives the universe a decidedly hostile bent. They believe that the race of life can never be won; that we are born to lose."

What do you think about death? What is your attitude towards this ultimate of endings? Do you avoid it, embrace it, value it, fear it or try not to think about it much? Do you believe in an after-life? If yes, what form do you believe this would take? Would you remember your life? If you had to put a percentage on how certain you are about this, what would the number be?[2]

An existential perspective on death holds that all of us are going to die. It is perhaps one of the only certainties in life, along with the fact that we will never know everything there is to know about the universe.[3] The problem is that we cannot know when and how we will die, only that it is going to happen (unless we take our own life). We are born and then we exist towards our body's inevitable demise. We are running out of life one breath at a time, so to speak without knowing how many breaths we got left. And regardless of our beliefs towards a soul, or any kind of afterlife, we know that our bodies die, and that is all we can really know for certain at this point.

Now we do not want to think about this fact every second of our exist-ence as it can be depressing and makes us feel anxious. But it also pro-vides us with a great source of energy to do and achieve the things that are meaningful to us. A round birthday (typically the time around our 30th and 50th) is often a time for meaningful change in people's lives. A near-death experience often leads people to radically change their ways in accordance with their values and beliefs. An illness, accident or death of a loved one may lead us to reconsider the ways in which we utilise our time on this planet. We tend to change the way we approach life when we realise profoundly that it can end at any moment; yet these changes tend to last for varying lengths of time as we slip back into our comfort-able ways.

But an awareness that everything ends (something Freud called transi-ence and many existentialists speak of as temporality, you may also call it impermanence of entropy[4]) can also be paralysing and de-motivating. What's the point in building something, investing into a relationship, entrepreneurial project or raising a child, when everything we know and love will inevitably die, potentially even much sooner that we had hoped for? "Would you rather have loved and lost or never loved at all?" is a question that many people answer with an affirmative of the latter as to avoid the pain of endings. Would you rather have lived and suffered or never lived at all? Suicide is often the conclusion of taking the latter stance at times when the suffering seems too great to bear and a person seems unable to focus on the good times that lay behind them and are likely to re-emerge in the future. How can we find meaning in our work when ultimately everything we work for decays and ends?

Helping our clients to adopt a mindset that focuses on the process of living rather than ultimate outcomes and embracing endings as a powerful source of meaning for any process is part of the work of an existential coach. If we were to live forever, then each day had less value, and therefore meaning. Why do anything today when you have an eternity to get things done? Why enjoy this moment when there is an infinite number of moments still to come? How could we take pleasure in a meal if it was to last for the rest of our lives? Even the best concert, film or show loses its appeal beyond a certain amount of time. Endings, and death as the ultimate ending, are crucial to our experience of the world. And exploring our clients' relationship with time and temporality is hence an important element of existential work.

Take a moment

A client's relationship with time can be related to many issues that are brought into coaching. For example, birthdays act as a reminder that time is ticking away and clients may find themselves procrastinating or working frantically as a result. A range of other behaviours may manifest as a result. Can you identify some of them? What is your own relationship with time and what kind of behaviours have you noticed in yourself?

Social dimension – isolation and "the other"

We are social animals. Humans have an innate need to relate. We always exist in relation to others. We naturally compare ourselves to others. We feel good when we are better than others (by our standards). Yet others also remind us of what we lack. We want both to belong, to be as similar as possible (not to be in conflict), and also to be a unique individual, to be different (which leads to conflict, not necessarily in the form of an argument or physical confrontation, but as differences in values, beliefs, opinions or worldview). Existentially, therefore, all human beings are in conflict with each other due to their uniqueness and individual differences. And while this necessarily creates conflict (even though we try our best not to let this escalate into violence) it is in essence a positive thing that helps us grow.

Illustrating the necessity of conflict for growth, German philosopher Hegel (1812) outlined the dialectic principles behind any such process. He argued that in order transcend (move forward) any idea, we necessarily need to synthesise a thesis and an opposing antithesis, meaning that without conflict between one idea and an opposing one we cannot really grow beyond either and things stay static. By this logic we need other people to disagree with us in order to grow ideas and we need other people to be different in order to grow as people. Democratic governments work in the same way (the governing body and the opposition are in constant debate, which helps to synthesise new ideas).

But again, this is not a comfortable process since, as human beings, we are hard-wired to connect with others. Thousands of years ago we needed to be around others to survive. Being banned from the group meant certain death. Therefore, through evolution we developed a strong urge to belong, to be part of a group, and the more similar we are the more we like each other. While we can appreciate that people who are very different to us (those who criticise us, disagree with us or have opposing political beliefs) help us grow as people, we crave harmony and piece and therefore tend to spend time among those with similar values, interests and socio-political backgrounds, we consume news media outlets that are in line without belief system and we often avoid situations that are likely to lead to confrontation of any kind.

Sartre (1944) famously stated that "Hell is other people", meaning that other people remind us of our existential isolation. And Orson Welles, interviewed in *Someone to Love* (dir. Jaglom, 1987), said, "We're born alone, we live alone, we die alone." At a fundamental level, we can never aspire to be the same as somebody else (even though many of us will have tried in our first romantic relationship). Other people are different, and so encountering them reminds us of our "otherness". Welles went on to note that "only through our love and friendship can we create the illusion for the moment that we're not alone." We long to ease this feeling of existential isolation through relationships, and we often seem to be happiest during times of positive illusions (such as wearing the rose-tinted glasses of infatuation). However, existentialists will prefer a relationship in which they are able to see their partner's dark sides, accepting them and embracing these, not as flaws, but as an inevitable part of the whole. Existential coaches see their clients in the same way and help them to do the same.

Take a moment

Think about your life in this context. Who are your friends? Which media outlets do you get your news from? Where do you go to socialise? Where did you travel to on your last five holidays and how did you spend your time there? What is your attitude towards conflict, debate, arguments and disputes? Are you vocal about your opinion in situations in which this would likely lead to conflict? Do you tell your friends what you think even if this may offend them? Are you challenging your clients' views, opinion and beliefs when you see a flaw in them or you disagree? How does your attitude affect your life?

Psychological dimension – authenticity and identity

At a personal level, we build an identity and a map of who we are and what we are like – our past experiences, our future possibilities, our character, our strengths, values, beliefs and what's important to us, characterised. These are characterised by the thoughts, feelings and visual imagery generated in our brain. Our sense of self is a product of what we have learned in life and how we made sense of our experiences. The people who provide us with explanations, expectations or who help us make sense of the world (first and foremost our primary caregivers but gradually they don't even have to be physically around us – think celebrities, writers and political figures) are a crucial element in this process.

Once we have created a world view and a sense of self that feels sufficiently coherent, authentic and in line with the kind of person we would like to be, we hold on to this framework and use it to guide future decisions. However, authenticity and a coherent worldview is not something we can achieve and then hold on to it for the rest of our lives. The world and all people within it change constantly. New information emerges every day. It is impossible to stay static. Even the happiest relationship (which includes your relationship with yourself) will start to feel boring if it does not grow and develop. So we need to keep our worldview and sense of self flexible and open to change, grow and develop as we moved into an uncertain future. The problem is that due to this uncertainty, changing is an uncomfortable process and a human instinct is to make sense of things and then hold on to what we know. Knowing things (who we are and how the world works) makes us feel safe.

Therefore, we often cling to our sense of self, even when we do things that may be at odds with this view. For example, we may cheat on a partner despite considering ourselves honest and trustworthy. We keep the lucrative business relationship with a supplier, despite having found out that they are treating their employees unethically. We complain about politics but we do not vote. We hate it when people lie and yet lie fairly frequently (or at least knowingly bend the facts in our or somebody else's favour). We think of ourselves as environmentally conscious but use plastic bottles and drive petrol cars. Somebody asks "How are you?" and we say "Great!" even though we are having a difficult day. We may behave one way with friends and very differently with colleagues at work or someone we are courting romantically, and then find ourselves in a situation where these groups mix (such as a birthday party or meeting somebody while out shopping in the city).

Often we are not quite aware of these behaviours as we naturally try to preserve a coherent self-image and hence rather not take any notice. When we are confronted with them (being called a hypocrite, somebody pointing out how we lied or acted dishonestly or a loved one or friend expressing hurt or surprise at one of our comments or actions) we can get defensive in an attempt to protect our sense of self. We deny or suppress what happened, warp our memory, or to explain it away in a way that fits in with who we (supposedly) are ("I was only lying to protect them", "my business's purpose is more important than the suffering of a few", "the voting system is rigged anyway"). If we do not manage to defend, deny or suppress this incoherence, we are left with food for thought and reflection, which may plunge us into a small (or sometimes big) crisis as a result of this inner conflict with regard to authenticity (depending on the gravity of the incident).

The existential coach is aware that due to the ever-changing nature of the world, people can never become fully authentic and then stay that way. We will inevitably weave in and out of authentic states as we go through life and continuously discover new blind spots as we evolve as people. We are always in a process of becoming.[5]

It takes a lot of effort to stay who you are and ultimately you set yourself up for failure if you try. The paradox on the psychological dimension is that we strive to be a coherent authentic whole while constantly changing. The best we can therefore strive for is to weave in and out of authenticity without straying too far away from who we are. And such a process requires continuous, honest and often uncomfortable reflection, an openness to critical feedback and exposing ourselves regularly to people who think differently about us. And even then we are bound to experience anxiety as for every noble idea you have, there is probably a person in the world who thinks you are a despicable human being for even thinking it. Again, the existential solution is to move forward despite this fact, rather than avoiding those who disagree with what we think is right and wrong or suppress the fact that they exist.

The existential coach is aware of the above and will therefore help their clients to identify areas of incongruence, willing to challenge their clients' thoughts and actions in the context of their self-image, even if this may be uncomfortable for them. The coach is willing to challenge and to face the discomfort together with the client in an understanding that it will allow them to correct their path towards what feels congruent with their beliefs, to right a wrong shortly after it happened and hence to stay as authentic as possible, rather than having to cure a personal identity crisis later down the line.

Take a moment

Authenticity is not a permanent state that we can achieve. We slip in and out of it. What have you done lately that felt authentic or inauthentic, and why? Reflect on the underlying elements in your worldview that contributed to the feeling of authenticity or inauthenticity. Similarly, when was the last time you identified an incongruence in a client's or friend's behaviour in the context of what they claim is important and meaningful to them? Did you challenge them at the time? What was their reaction? If they became defensive or even aggressive, what could you do as to ensure them that you challenged them in their best interest?

Spiritual dimension – meaning and purpose

Human beings are meaning-making machines. It is our natural instinct to try and make sense of what we experience. Consider, for example, Figure 3.1: there is no triangle. Likewise Figure 3.2: that is not a face. Your brain added this information.

It is evolutionarily hard-wired into our brains to make sense of things quickly and to learn how our world operates. It helped us survive and it still does. That is why we are born curious. One of the most irritating things that can happen to us is when we cannot understand something

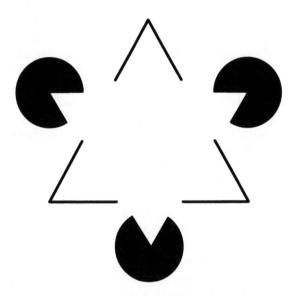

Figure 3.1 Three incomplete circles and three lines bent at an angle create the illusion of two triangles emerging in their midst.

Figure 3.2 Two dots and the letter "D" on its side create the illusion of a face.

that affects us deeply, when something seems absurd, mind-boggling. As touched on above, these are the situations where our worldview, our conceptual map of how the world works and which we worked so hard to create, is being attacked. It can even drive some people mad when they encounter something that does not fit into their worldview and they may work for decades to prove the world wrong (rather than to adjust their own theory or accept that sometimes the world may simply be absurd).

French existentialist writer Camus (1946) describes a "stranger" to whom the whole world seems absurd, which leads him to disengage from much of what we would call a human experience (characterised by care for others and a meaning greater than merely existing). The stranger simply does not seem to care about anything, including his mother's death, getting married, killing a man, going to prison or even his own death sentence. He does not submit to social norms and instead honestly and courageously follows his own subjective experience to guide him through the world. It is a compelling argument that there is no one overarching universal objective meaning *of* life and that we can only ever attach meaning to things *in* our life, based on subjective or societal norms. And even if there was a life-script, a master plan or such thing as destiny, all of which would provide our existence with meaning and purpose from the outside, nobody has ever found any universally accepted evidence for such a claim, nor is it likely that anybody will ever be able to do so. We can merely have faith in it or choose to believe in such an explanation for why things happen or why we exist.

The most philosophically sound explanation from an existential philosophical point of view is that existence is absurd, that meaninglessness (or rather the impossibility for a human being to grasp such meaning) is one of the givens of being alive.

At first sight a rather depressing-sounding viewpoint (and in fact often misinterpreted as such), inherent in such a conclusion lies an enormous freedom: If there are no rules (but rather only those we create for ourselves or choose to adopt and follow) then we are ultimately free to do whatever we want (as long as we are willing to accept the consequences of our actions within a world that we may not be able to control). If there was a script and we are the puppets than whatever we do is what we were meant to do anyway. Camus's stranger chose to travel his path, guided by his subjective experience, and to face the consequences of his actions. He showed courage and authenticity in doing so.

An existential coach will provide a place where their clients can choose to do the same. And while the stranger's fate ends in his demise (as a novelist Camus depicts an extreme example), the existentialist would rather suffer as a consequence of standing up for what is meaningful to them than to submit to any dogma or norms that they disagree with (or at least accept the consequences of choosing not to do so – such as choosing to continue an unfulfilling job for the sake of feeding their children, a choice that in turn provides meaning to that very job and hence can be re-framed as fulfilling through the process of exploring this situation in great depth in the coaching room).

Even at a much smaller level it is useful to stay open to and sit with the often uncomfortable feeling that surrounds meaninglessness. New information that does not make sense within our current understanding, and hence challenges the accuracy of our map of meanings, is an opportunity to grow and develop, an invitation to reconsider and adjust our worldview and allow it to transcend into a more complete understanding of the world. In the short term it may be more comfortable to disregard or reject such information instead of spending valuable resources (time and energy) to consider them carefully, especially when we had already formed what we see as a coherent view and understanding. However, let us assume that our understanding of the world was limited (as it so often happens). With time it will become increasingly difficult to reject the new and more suitable view. However, the more resources one had previously invested in their view (such as for example having published books on the topic, formed a company around the premise or having argued passionately in public) the harder it will be to let it go, amend it or replace it. Sometimes it gets to a point where people make themselves believe even the most ridiculous explanation (which to be fair seemed reasonable at the time of formation) in order to at least *have* an explanation or not to have to let go of what they have built.[6]

In order to avoid admitting that we have been wrong, finding the courage to apologise to someone or invest more time and energy into changing our views or rebuild our worldview, we often use self-deception in order to protect ourselves from the discomfort this entails. This process may be conscious (avoiding certain people or quiet time for reflection) or unconscious (such as bad faith). When we are being confronted with situation in which we are forced to see our double standards or can no longer deny that our meaning map has cracks (or even a gaping hole that we did not allow ourselves to see), we tend to get emotional, which can lead to a whole range of challenging behaviours.

It happens all the time and all levels of existence (from big questions around the meaning of existence to rather mundane issues such as the two images above): we often try to find meaning even where they may be none. It is difficult to accept absurdity and meaninglessness when we are hard-wired for making meaning while at the same time we cannot reject this notion using logic and reason. We can only choose (or sometimes perhaps *find*) what feels meaningful to us *personally*, and embrace that this will differ from other people's perspectives. And that this is ultimately what makes life worth living (imagine we all accepted the same views, rules, knowledge and meanings, what would be left to talk about?).

An existential coach will help their clients explore their map of meanings and beliefs (ranging from personal and subjective, via factual and objective explanations, to situational, social, spiritual or cosmic meanings) and to check in with these regularly in relation to what they experience in day-to-day existence. Not only does this build existential resilience against future crises by encouraging continuous exploration and hence prevent the client from straying too far from reality, it also allows the client to make decisions based on a well-considered framework of their world and what is important to them personally (such as how to best spend their time or how to respond to a conflict or important decision).

Take a moment

Write about a few things that feel meaningful to you personally. This may be something that just feels right when you do it, something that you believe is worth suffering for, or something that you decide has a meaningful effect on the world (as a whole or any specific part of it). It may be an outcome, an activity, a process or anything else you assign meaning to.

How would you help a client to explore their meaning framework? Some ask direct questions aimed at uncovering underlying beliefs to behaviours (write down a couple of these). Others let them emerge freely from the conversation and keep a mental map. What is your preferred approach?

Boundary situations

Time and again, we find ourselves in situations that confront us with one or a number of the above-mentioned paradoxes. At these so-called "boundary situations", existential feelings and questions break through our layers of self-deception (our defence against existential anxiety) and force our eyes open to catch a glimpse of the paradoxes of being. In these situations, our personal, individual existence leaves us vulnerable, and with no choice but to temporarily feel the existential angst. These situations may last just a moment, or they may stay with a person for some time. When they are prolonged, we may speak of an existential crisis, to which a boundary situation may have been the trigger.

Triggers might be small things that remind us that we do not live forever (such as lump in the chest, a birthday or an illness), or they may come in the form of profound incisions into our worldview (such as a near-death experience, a relationship breakup taking us by surprise or getting fired unexpectedly). As much as we may try to protect ourselves from existential anxiety, it is almost inevitable that sooner or later we will be confronted with our existential concerns (for example, it is a mere matter of time until we are reminded that death exists, either by encountering the death of friends or, ultimately, approaching our own demise). Our ability to suppress these realities can be incredibly strong, yet we all experience these boundary situations at least momentarily.

The existential coach welcomes these circumstances as an invitation to reconsider life and the way we live it. The stronger the feeling of discomfort we feel in these situations, the clearer the indication that we have been avoiding or denying some important aspect of our existence. It is important at these times to create time for reflection and to sit with these feelings for some time as to explore what triggered them including their underlying assumptions as to be able to correct the course towards a more authentic and considered relationship with the world and the self.

Edgar Lee Masters (1915, p. 64) expressed the paradox of meaning well when he wrote in one of his poems: "To put meaning in one's life may end in madness, but life without meaning is the torture of restlessness and vague desire; It is a boat longing for the sea and yet afraid."

Take a moment

For each of the four dimensions described above, describe a boundary situation from your personal life experience or your coaching work in which you (or a client) were confronted with an existential conflict. This would have been a time when self-deception broke down abruptly, or when faced with a dilemma. See below for some examples:

- Physical – a near-death experience.
- Psychological – a line manager, passionate as well as financially dependent on their job, being ordered to enforce a course of action that they strongly disagree with.
- Social – a teenager, aware of the risks of smoking as well as holding their social status in the group to high esteem, being peer-pressured by their friends.
- Spiritual – a believer in the Illuminati conspiracy seeing the number 23 everywhere or a devoted believer in the Old Testament being confronted with their son's homosexual preferences.

Uncertainty

Nothing in this world is certain. Perhaps we might even find a cure for mortality. Time and again what was thought to be impossible is demonstrated to be possible. A man with amputated legs competes in the Olympics as a runner (Oscar Pistorius), a black man becomes president of the United States of America (Barack Obama), an ear is grown on the back of a mouse (Cervantes et al., 2013), we've seen a triple backflip being performed on a bicycle (Gavin Godfrey), Germany beat Brazil 7–1 in the 2014 Football World Cup, and somebody who made a simple plan to leave his house and go to work failed to achieve his goal due a heart attack.

We simply never know with 100 per cent certainty that something will or won't happen. Yet we have a tendency to make decisions only once we are certain of a desirable outcome. As a result, we experience anxiety whenever we face a decision as we can never truly know whether we are making the right choice. We can only make assumptions based on statistics, experience, intuition, probability or other factors that are more or less, but never fully reliable. A base level of anxiety due to this uncertainty always remains and is an inevitable part of human existence. And this applies to small decision such as which would be the best lunch option as well as to forks in the road, decisions that may change the course of our lives forever.

The positive perspective on this uncertainty is that it also makes life worth living. Indeed human beings seek it out to make life more exciting and thrilling. We tend not to read the last page of a book first; we don't want to know the outcome of a sports game that we are passionate about before we have watched it; and, if we could know the exact time when we will die, much of life's magic would be lost. People enjoy crime novels and films where the outcome is uncertain, and many people even watch horror movies that deliberately make them feel uncomfortable. We seek this feeling of uncertainty because it's the very stuff that makes us feel alive.

Take a moment

Write about some of the pros and cons of uncertainty. Give examples of when you have sought it out and when you tried to make it go away.

Often, our most memorable moments in life, the exciting stories we tell others, are challenges and knotty situations in which we had to make difficult, perhaps seemingly impossible, choices; situations in which life threw us a curveball and challenged us, sometimes to the very core of our being; or situations in which we may have faced death or serious adversity, when our life was at a crossroads and could have taken a significant turn. At times, we imagine how our lives would have turned out if we had chosen this or that course of action instead of another.

When we tell people about these kinds of situations with pride, we usually take credit for having made a certain decision or chosen a particular course of action. But sometimes we don't get that sense of accomplishment; we don't feel as if we could take credit for what happened; we might feel that life just happened to us, rather than our playing an active part in it. We are talking about responsibility and accountability here, something that many people claim or reject based on perceived positive or negative outcomes. Your clients might claim they got lucky out of an unhelpful sense of modesty, or they may take false credit for circumstances that were in fact beyond their control.

While we can utilise different forms of explanatory style (see Buchanan and Seligman, 2013) in order to influence our mood, feelings, thoughts and behaviour, the existential coach would encourage their client to become aware of their attitude towards responsibility as this enables them to make conscious, authentic decisions in line with their values and beliefs. We want our clients not to deceive themselves by taking false credit for a short-lived sense of happiness. We want them to have their eyes as fully open as possible, and to face life's challenges courageously and authentically, and then take full credit and responsibility for what they did and what they chose not to do.

The existential view is that human beings are "condemned to be free" (Sartre, 1946), which beautifully expresses the paradox of *getting* to choose and *having* to choose at the same time. It means that we are free to choose whatever we want (as long as we are prepared to live with whatever consequences this may carry), that everything is allowed (because every person ultimately chooses to follow certain rules or make up their own) but that at the same time we cannot reject personal responsibility of our actions and inactions. In our need for certainty and harmony we often fall into following existing sets of rules (social, societal, legal or else), accepting dogma (e.g. what our parents teach us or religious texts dictate), but existentialists call for challenging dogma and encourage people to make their own rules.

Dostoevsky wrote: "If God did not exist, everything would be permitted" (cited in Sartre's famous lecture from 1946) and for existentialists, that is the starting point. We are free to do whatever we want, yet we also *have* to choose and live with the consequences of what we do and don't do. Therefore, every choice we make causes a certain amount of anxiety. And Heidegger (1971) wrote powerfully: "Freedom is not a property of man; man is the property of freedom."

Take a moment

Think about a few situations in your life in which you have rejected personal responsibility or not given yourself enough credit for your involvement. Then think about a situation in which you may have rejected accountability but later had to admit to yourself that you at least shared some of the responsibility. What is your attitude towards responsibility and how could you use it in your coaching work?

Decision making and dilemmas

Many clients come to coaching with a difficult decision that they are currently struggling with and almost always, difficult decisions emerge at some point during the coaching.[7] Many of these decisions (particularly the big and important ones) are linked to existential themes, particularly choice, responsibility and uncertainty. Important or difficult choices are usually linked to what's important to us, our worldview, beliefs and values. Difficulty in making decisions can stem from conflicting needs or wants and existentially there are many such inner conflicts.

Furthermore, we make thousands of decisions every single day, from when and how to get up in the morning and what to eat to bigger decisions that may affect the rest of our lives and potentially many other people's lives. Sometimes we cannot see how our actions affect our future or other people and how the future will turn out is inherently uncertainly. We became pretty good at making predictions and logical conclusions about the future but we will never be able to predict human behaviour fully.

Existentially, the anxiety and discomfort that accompany decision making stem from two sources: Firstly, every choice we make excludes other possibilities. If we choose A, we will never be able to choose A at this time again. We may change our mind and choose B instead but even if this happens almost instantaneous, it will never be the same as choosing A immediately and without hesitation.

For example, if we choose to be with a certain romantic partner, we are excluding many (or all depending on where you stand on monogamy) others. Even if we are very happy with our current partner, we will never know whether a different partner may have not led us to be even happier. This inevitable uncertainty is something that everybody has to live with. But because it is uncomfortable (and indeed very painful to some), it is an understandable urge to bridge such uncertainty by choosing to believe in certain outcomes despite not being able to be sure (e.g. we're soulmates, we were destined to be with each other, or it was decided by our parents). "Taking a leap of faith" is an expression that Kierkegaard termed when he talked about bridging the existential uncertainty and courageously moving forward in life despite doubts and uncomfortable feelings.

The second source of anxiety is about responsibility and accountability. As soon as we choose we are ultimately responsible for the consequences of our actions (or inactions). While many things in this world are beyond our control and we can only choose to the best of our knowledge at any given time, many people shy away from making decisions in order to avoid the responsibility that comes with them. This may lead to a range of symptoms such as procrastination, lack of motivation, stress, even personal crises etc.

For example, a client may not quit their job in pursuit of going freelance as they do not want to risk their regular pay check and the security that it provides despite the opportunity of making a lot more money and following their dreams. They may be worried about the people who are financially dependant on them (e.g. their family) or perhaps they have a hard time forgiving themselves for mistakes or failure.

The existential coach will explore and reflect back such situations and the client's worldview in a broader context so that they may make the relevant connections and better understand their choices and what leads to them. When seemingly impossible choices are explored in such a way and the client makes meaningful connections between the dilemma at hand and their unique way of being in the world with others, the client is often able to understand what's at stake. In an understanding that not-choosing is a choice in itself and that we are "condemned to be free", meaning that we cannot *not* choose, it is often easier to make a choice, to bear the existential dread that comes with it and perhaps even start to embrace the excitement that the future's uncertainty entails (remember that most of us don't really want to know how the book that we're reading ends, or at least we don't skip ahead. We appreciate the journey. After all, it's what we paid for).

Once a client develops a broader awareness of the context within which they are being faced with difficult decisions or dilemmas (their personal and unique existential worldview) and with an understanding that sometimes there simply aren't any *right* or *wrong* choices – just *choices* – an authentic way forward emerges.

Take a moment

Describe a situation from your life or with a client, in which you or they felt unable to make a choice, which then became much easier to make through a process of exploration. Try to connect this to the relevant existential themes that the choice entailed.

A note on religion

Most religions offer solutions to existential anxieties by offering ideology as to what comes after death, answers to big questions (certainty), meaning, guidance and a sense of belonging and togetherness, usually grounded in an unquestionable (as in impossible to be questioned or falsified) belief, or faith in an infinite, all-knowing, all-powerful and ever-present deity.

It is therefore a common misconception that existentialists are also atheist. While many secular existentialists indeed do not believe in a deity (perhaps most prominently Nietzsche, who exclaimed that "God is dead") and suggest that we instead choose our own meaning in an existence that is characterised by an overarching absurdity and meaninglessness, many existential thinkers had and have a strong connection to God, perhaps not as depicted in a book but rather through a deep and personal connection with something greater than themselves.

Kierkegaard was a devoted Christian and though he did not speak highly of the organised church (which was and still is the epitome of upholding dogma and not known to be particularly open to challenge), he had a strong personal relationship with his God and indeed this was one of the pillars of his philosophy. Other notable Christian existentialists were Paul Tillich, Rollo May, Karl Jaspers, Gabriel Mercer and Karl Barth. The main tenet of Christian existential thought is that we cannot find a relationship with god outside of us (by doing things like going to church or other religious practice), but rather that it is through being, through grappling with life's big questions that we can find a relationship with God within us as we realise that there is no distance between ourselves as individuals and the world at large (see Buber's I–Thou relationships).

Other religions (with the exception of Judaism and the writings of Martin Buber and Victor Frankl) have not produced outspokenly existential thinkers or works of literature, presumably due to the fact that it primarily spawned in Europe and the US.

The existential coach will not encourage an atheistic worldview (even if the coach believes strongly in the non-existence of God or gods). Keep in mind that we can neither prove nor disprove the existence of such an entity and atheism therefore remains just as much a *belief* as religious faith does. However, the existential coach will likely have a conversation with their clients about how they relate to the world at the spiritual dimension and challenge their them on some of their ideas and beliefs so that they may either become stronger through the process of exploration or they may build a worldview and belief system that is more suitable to who they are, their environment and how they choose to live their lives (and this could go either way, towards or away from a concept of God).

Existential "solutions"

Faced with existential concerns, your clients may ask: What can I do to overcome or transcend this existential anxiety? How can I alleviate the pain and suffering that results from my human condition? How can you help me to overcome my fears and resolve these inner conflicts so that I can live a better life and be happy? Well, to begin with we need to ask the right questions in the context of what you have learned above.

While many forms of anxiety can be alleviated or resolved, existential anxiety is not something that we can eliminate. The only way to transcend the human condition is, by definition, to stop being human, to stop existing. The inner conflicts that we experience as a result of being alive and in the world with others cannot be overcome, at best we can suppress it by means of distraction or by avoiding periods of stillness and reflection. But as we have also noted above, this may bear a number of undesirable consequences in the long-term. And even if one were to somehow succeed in not getting entangled in any boundary situations until the day of a very sudden death, the question remains whether this is a desirable way to live life.

I know my answer to this question, and again, would not judge someone who chooses comfort over suffering in exchange for seeing existence for what it is (after all the is arguable bliss in ignorance). But for those who aspire to understand their life and relations in existential terms, the only solution is to live in spite of their human condition ("trotzdem"). Paul Tillich (1952), one of the most prominent theologians of the twentieth century, referred to this as developing "the courage to be" in the face of meaninglessness. He advocated to get in touch with the sheer power of being. In times of suffering, we are reminded that we exist, as there could not be any suffering without being. Once we accept, or resign to, this paradoxical relationship we can live with what he called absolute faith. Kierkegaard, in the late nineteenth century, similarly advocated to take a "leap of faith" into the human condition. Personally, having spent my teenage years immersed in the hip-hop culture of the 1990s find meaning in my human suffering knowing that I am indeed "keeping it real" (or rather weaving in and out of realness as best as I can). The metaphorical "red pill" from the popular movie *The Matrix* (1999) is another example from contemporary culture, in which the protagonist chooses to rather face the bleak and challenging reality of a futuristic world in which robots are close to bringing the human race to extinction rather than taking the "blue pill" and waking up after a bad dream back in a safe, but meaningless computer simulation.

Of course, not everybody is a courageous hero, or chooses to be. But regardless of our attitude towards courage, risk and facing anxiety and meaninglessness, only if we allow ourselves to look into the abyss can we choose whether or not to jump. And those who choose to look (and thereby face their anxieties) are heroes to the existentialist, "knights of faith" as Kierkegaard so beautifully wrote:

> When around one everything has become silent, solemn as a clear, starlit night, when the soul comes to be alone in the whole world, then before one there appears, not an extraordinary human being, but the eternal power itself, then the heavens open, and the I chooses itself or, more correctly, receives itself. Then the personality receives the accolade of knighthood that ennobles it for an eternity.
>
> (Kierkegaard, 1843/1987, p. 177)

Elsewhere he wrote that "the knight of faith is the only happy man, the heir to the finite while the knight of resignation is a stranger and an alien" (Kierkegaard, 1843/1983, p. 50).

Therefore, an existentially aware client does have to radically change their lives from an outsider's perspective (such as quitting their job and starting their own business) in order to be a hero, as long as they will have allowed themselves, courageously, to become aware of their freedom, consider their options, choose not to live in bad faith and bear the suffering of their human condition and the consequences of their inactions with grace and acceptance. After all there is no right way to live and quitting their job may have been a terrible idea after all. It is not about the way we live our lives, but to choose our path consciously despite the givens. In accepting the uncertainty of the world and the consequences of our actions (as far as we are able to grasp them at the time) we are able choose confidently, as in the act of choosing we find life itself.

Take a moment

What could you do today to face life more courageously? In which areas of your life have you consciously chosen comfort over challenge (rather than making excuses)?

A number of other existential "solutions"[8] have been formulated. For example, van Deurzen (1996, 2014) advocates an awareness of truth and to develop existential intelligence, which she summarised as:

- Embracing existence in its contradictions and rising to its challenges.
- Realizing that there is no such thing as a perfect human being.
- Learning to be resilient and flexible enough to negotiate ongoing paradoxes.
- Facing existential challenges in a personal and creative manner that allows for dialectic.

(van Deurzen, 1996, p. 202)

Nietzsche argues for choosing a purpose, or life project, to connect to something larger than ourselves, which in turn provides meaning *in* life (rather than attempting to find an overarching meaning *of* life). He stated that "if we have our own why in life, we shall get along with almost any how" (Nietzsche 1889/1990, §1.12), later echoed by Frankl's (1963, p. 111) perhaps more popular "he who has a why to live for can bear almost any how".

Buber (1937) highlighted the importance of the way we relate to others and the world as we experience it. He argued that the only way we can truly meet the world is to relate to otherness not as an object (I–It) and hence objectify people, experiences, objects and so on (such as using them as a means to an end), but to acknowledge a living relationship with who or whatever we come into contact with (I–Thou), to merge the distance between us and the world around us, to view us and the world as one and hence be better able to positively relate to being and suffering.

Spinelli (1997), an existential therapist-turned-coach, and perhaps the first to write about coaching as a means to working existentially (certainly the first to train and supervise existential coaches in his school in London), promotes, as you may have guessed, a process of exploration, and hence understanding as a pathway to live better.

A noteworthy, recent emergence is the second wave of positive psychology – also referred to as Positive Psychology 2.0, or PP2.0 – a term coined by Wong (2010) and further described by my colleagues from the University of East London (Ivtzan, Lomas, Hefferon & Worth, 2016). Traditionally concerned only with the study of what is *right* with people (such as character strengths, positive emotions, conceptualisations of happiness and wellbeing as well as interventions aimed at increasing flourishing of individuals and groups), this second wave of researchers embraced the dialectic nature of individuals and the world and hence argued that any theory of wellbeing will be incomplete without embracing the dark side of life.

Take a moment

Which "solutions" have you already implemented? Which ones could you work to develop and how? Can you think of a client who may benefit from learning about a particular school of thought? How may you bring the above to their attention?

Notes

1 This is part of the reason why flow states are so desirable. When we are in flow (some call it "in the zone" or optimal experience) we are completely immersed in and absorbed by an activity to a point where we lose our sense of time, we do not feel anything (good or bad) or are aware of any thoughts or stimuli that are not directly related to the activity at hand. Every moment flows to the next and often people perform at their best in these states. Flow states occur when a number of conditions are met, most importantly that the challenge of the activity is in line with our skill level and that we are intrinsically motivated to engage with it (rather than as a means to an end). People report a feeling of bliss, not during, but after a flow experience as they were not concerned with anything outside this space (including their human condition, future problems, past pains or any feelings at all). However, these states are not sustainable and attempting to create them on an ongoing basis has negative consequences. I

recommend Csíkszentmihályi (2008) and Kotler (2014) if you'd like to learn more about flow.

2 Thanks to Pollen (2018) for reporting being asked this question by Prof. Roland Griffiths, as it forces people to think more deeply about an often loosely held belief about death such as this. The existential coach aspires to invite clients to think more deeply about their assumptions as to help clients build a more solid worldview in the process.

3 Though who knows where we stand on this in a couple of billion years – if we make it that far. Even today, bio-technology is developing faster than exponentially and it thinkable that we may someday find a way to sustain the human body indefinitely through cell-regeneration or some other way. So far there is no evidence for a half-life of the human mind (an expiry date so to speak).

4 I recommend watching the philosopher and filmmaker Jason Silva speak about the "existential bummer" to illustrate this notion, available on his YouTube channel "Shots of Awe".

5 A quote often attributed to Bruce Lee's character in the movie *Enter the Dragon* (1973), but widely used by those who have realised that human beings cannot be static.

6 Comedian and existential thinker Bill Hicks famously exclaimed at the end of each of his shows that "It's just a ride!" ("it" meaning "life"), and points out how so many people seem to be unable to accept that life is ultimately absurd since they have "a lot invested in this ride", which in turn makes it very difficult to understand how some people do not seem to take life very seriously.

7 Here's a profound exchange I had during a retreat once:

Me: "I came here for answers, yet all I found is more questions."

Him (smiles): "Good. Let's talk about it."

8 I keep using speech marks when I talk about existential "solutions" as by definition these are not solutions for existential anxiety or the human condition (the only way to transcend the human condition is not to be human and therefore to stop existing), but rather ways to deal with or embrace the human condition and to live life in despite its inevitable challenges.

References

Binswanger, L. (1963). *Being in the World*. New York: Basic Books.

Buber, M. (1937). *I and Thou*. London: Continuum.

Buchanan, G.M., & Seligman, M.E.P. (2013). *Explanatory Style*. Hillsdale, NJ: Erlbaum.

Camus, A. (1946). *The Stranger* (trans. S. Gilbert). New York: Alfred Knopf.

Canning, B. (2007). *The Death Delusion*. Retrieved from https://bardcan.word press.com/2007/08/25/thoughts-on-the-toughest-questions-we-face

Cervantes, T.M., Basset, E.K., Tseng, A., Kimura, A., et al. (2013). Design of composite scaffolds and three-dimensional shape analysis for tissue-engineered ear. *Interface*, *10*(87). Retrieved from http://rsif.royalsocietypub lishing.org/content/10/87/20130413

Cooper, M. (2003). *Existential Therapies*. London: Sage.

Csíkszentmihályi, M. (2008). *Flow: The Psychology of Optimal Experience*. New York: Harper Perennial.

Frankl, V. (1963). *Man's Search for Meaning*. New York: Pocket Books.

Hegel, G.W.F. (1812). *The Science of Logic* (vol. 1; trans. W.H. Johnston & L.G. Struthers). New York: The Macmillan Company.

Heidegger, M. (1962). *Being and Time* (trans. J. Macquarie & E. Robinson). New York: Basic Books.

Heidegger, M. (1971). *Schelling's Treatise on the Essence of Human Freedom* (trans. J. Stambaugh). Athens, OH: Ohio University Press.

Ivtzan, I., Lomas, T., Worth, P., & Hefferon, K. (2016). *Second Wave Positive Psychology: Embracing the Dark Side of Life*. London: Routledge.

Kierkegaard, S. (1843/1983). *Fear and Trembling* (trans. H.V. Hong and E.H. Hong). Princeton, NJ: Princeton University Press.

Kierkegaard, S. (1843/1987). *Either/Or* (vol. 2; trans. H. Hong & E. Hong). Princeton, NJ: Princeton University Press.

Kotler, S. (2014). *The Rise of Superman: Decoding the Science of Ultimate Human Performance*. New York: Houghton, Mifflon, Harcourt.

Masters, E.L. (1915). *Spoon River Anthology*. New York: Macmillan.

Nietzsche, F. (1889/1990). *Twilight of the Idols* (trans. R.J. Hollingdale). London: Penguin Books.

Pollen, M. (2018). *How to Change Your Mind: The New Science of Psychedelics*. London: Allen Lane.

Sartre, J.-P. (1944). *No Exit*. New York: Vintage Books.

Sartre, J.-P. (1946). Existentialism is a humanism. Public lecture. Retrieved from www.marxists.org/reference/archive/sartre/works/exist/sartre.htm

Sartre, J.-P. (1958). *Being and Nothingness: An Essay in Phenomenological Ontology* (trans. H.E. Barnes). London: Routledge.

Spinelli, E. (1997). *Tales of Unknowing*. London: Duckworth.

Tillich, P. (1952). *The Courage to Be*. New Haven, CT: Yale University Press.

van Deurzen, E. (1996). *Everyday Mysteries: Existential Dimensions of Psychotherapy*. London: Routledge.

van Deurzen, E. (2014). Perspectives on psychological disturbance, happiness and emotional well being. Public Lecture, Aarhus, Denmark, May. Retrieved from www.slideshare.net/emmyzen/existential-perspectives-on-well-being

van Deurzen, E., & Hanaway, M. (2012). *Existential Perspectives on Coaching*. Basingstoke, UK: Palgrave Macmillan.

van Deurzen-Smith, E. (1984). Existential therapy. In W. Dryden (ed.), *Individual Therapy in Britain* (pp. 152–172). London: Harper & Row.

Wong, P.T.P. (2010). What is existential positive psychology? *International Journal of Existential Psychology and Psychotherapy*, *3*, 1–10.

Yalom, I. (1980). *Existential Psychotherapy*. New York: Basic Books.

Chapter 4

Existential coaching in practice

Laying the right foundations

Not every client will be open to discussing existential themes in a coaching framework. Due to the nature of the philosophy and the magnitude of its fundamental questions, clients may prefer to discuss these topics with themselves, among friends or in therapy. However, as mentioned above, an understanding of the human condition will inform your practice and your appreciation of the client as a whole, regardless of this being the issue that the client brought to discuss. Still, it is important to once more highlight that, even though you may have identified existential themes or dilemmas at the heart of a client's goal or challenge, it is always the client's choice to what extent they would like to engage in the subject matter.

For example, a client's tendency towards procrastination may be linked to their relationship with temporality and an avoidance of engaging fully with their existence; however, they may choose to develop behavioural strategies aimed at "just doing it" so as to, in turn, gradually influence their thoughts and habits towards a more productive version of themselves, rather than to address the underlying dissonance with their existential attitude towards time and their denial of their ultimate responsibility. There is no one right way of delivering great coaching and while, arguably, insights, shifts and changes at a deeper level tend to yield more sustainable results in the long-term, it is our client's choice as to what kind of support they are seeking. It is therefore crucial to lay the right foundations for existential work and contract clearly the extent to which an exploration of philosophical dimensions will inform your work together.

The contracting conversation (which will take place at the beginning of the work, yet needs to be kept going throughout the entire coaching relationship) is a crucial ethical component for the existentially minded coach. It is of utmost importance that the client makes an informed decision on how they choose to proceed and what they are agreeing to. Existential work can be very challenging. Facing life's challenges and anxieties and aiming to uncover one's blind spots in order to live fully and authentically can involve questions that are difficult to engage with. The client needs to have an understanding of this, along with the courage to engage in such an undertaking. In order to introduce the process and the basic tenets of existential practice, the models described in this section – in combination with your introduction of your personal approach – may help both you and the client to grasp what existential work is about, ultimately enabling them to make an informed decision on whether you are the right coach for them.

Phenomenological inquiry

Existential work is a process of exploration within the safety of a strong relationship (see Chapter 2). We create a space in which the client is encouraged to reflect on their goals, behaviours, experiences, conflicts, thoughts and emotions in relation to their broader world view and lived experience of being in this world. As such the main method or tool that is used in existential work is what we call "phenomenological inquiry".

Phenomenological inquiry is a method in which the coach temporarily suspends ("brackets") all their existing assumptions about a "phenomenon". These may be what we think we know a person (regardless of how sure we are or any consideration of what we may call "objective truths"), any hypotheses we may have about an outcome of a path of action or the cause of a situation, or any interpretation whatsoever of what is brought into the coaching space by the client during the duration of the inquiry. Everything a client says is being taken at face value, no matter how clear, ridiculous, logical, unrealistic, helpful, destructive (or whichever other label we may have normally attached to them) their words may be. During phenomenological enquiry (and yes, it takes a little while to master saying the word out loud), nothing is taken as self-explanatory, a process called horizontalisation. Pretend that you know nothing about the(ir) world.

For example, when a client says that they are feeling "good", do not assume that you know what this means. When a client reports that the likely outcome of a meeting will be disastrous, do not think that you share the same understanding of what "disastrous" entails. When they describe to you how punching somebody in the face is clearly the best solution to their problem, for the moment it may be most helpful to accept that this is your client's current reality and may, in fact, just be true. The result is that your client feels truly "tuned in" to and is able to hear themselves speak without interruption, correction or interpretation and allows the client to delve deeper into their own worldview, assumptions and beliefs.

Take a moment

Imagine you're an alien life form and you are looking at an object for the first time in your life (such as a raisin). Write down what you think it is for, what it is made of, where it came from, how it sounds, what it may taste like (assuming that it is edible) etc. Try to suspend everything you know about the object and to notice which things might still remain. Use all of your senses to explore.

Alternatively you could find a grocery store selling products from around the world and pick something up that you do not recognise. Go through the above process and then google it.

During phenomenological enquiry we try to avoid why-questions as these tend to force the client to make interpretations immediately (an automatic process that we are trying to circumvent as not to fall into familiar patterns of meaning-making). Instead we facilitate a process of description in an effort to open up space that will in turn allow for creating new interpretations and explanations.

Clients often jump to conclusions, particularly when they have long-held (or sedimented) assumptions or beliefs, which are often a core obstacle to what they are trying to achieve. By inviting them to describe their situation rather than interpreting it (through asking questions that typically begin with what, when and how) we facilitate a process of exploration, the clients hear themselves talk and often it is through this process alone that new possibilities and alternative solutions emerge.

At any point the coach may choose to "tune out" again, reconnect with their own worldview, knowledge and experience (including their toolbox, coaching approach, expertise, process or whatever else may guide their coaching work) and choose how to respond what the client has been expressing. However, often the mere act of tuning in fully produces insights in the client and the process continues.

The strength of the phenomenological approach is multi-faceted. First, a strong relationship is formed as the coach does not oppose or challenge the client at this stage and is only guided by their child-like curiosity. Challenges only emerge as clients bring themselves face to face with their own inner conflicts or incongruences. Hence the process is non-directive and the coach has no agenda other than to help the client explore whatever they introduced into the coaching room. As a result the client feels empowered as they arrive at insights while they are talking. It is not unusual for the coach to be amazed at how easily clients start accessing answers to their problems or pathways to their desires simply by tuning in to what it is they brought with a lot of curiosity and zero assumptions.

The difficulty of inquiring phenomenologically lies in the act of bracketing itself as it is never possible to be completely free from assumptions. As soon as we encounter a person or the beginning of a story (or even just part of a sentence), our brain automatically categorises the information in relation to what we already know and have experienced previously (see examples of meaning making on p. 43). Often, we form a number of assumptions within a few seconds. In everyday life, this is often a helpful process that allows us to make fast decisions and function efficiently in a fast-paced world; we would struggle considerably if we were not at least partly able to trust our assumptions and interpretations.

However, the existential coaching space is different. It is a place for deliberate exploration, a place where the client wants to identify patterns in their thinking and in the assumptions they make that result in them feeling stuck and at a loss for alternative ways forward – a place where they can challenge their unhelpful beliefs and assumptions. As such the phenomenological method of inquiry allows coach and client to go deeper into what it being brought into the coaching space.

While we will not succeed to bracket any and all assumptions, we can train ourselves to be as aware as possible when an assumption starts to trigger a response in us, and at that point to consciously bracket it. Think of this as taking said assumption, conclusion or a feeling invoked by an interpretation (such as a feeling of frustration arising as the client repeats themselves and an assumption that you know where they are going with this) and putting it into a mental box or on a mental shelf. Be aware that it exists, yet do not let it influence your next question, response or attitude towards your client. Bring yourself back into the present moment and fully tune in, rather than making sense of what is being said in the back of your mind or trying to connect it to what was said in previous sessions.[1]

Take a moment

Read the following sentences and write down all of the assumptions that come up for you. These may include images, thoughts, interpretations, colours, smells, explanations, outcomes, connections to people, experience, memories or anything else that comes to your mind.

Forty-two civilians died during the air raid.

Alex ran like hell.

I awkwardly bumped into her at the local supermarket.

I went in to work on Monday morning and was told to clear my desk.

I'm fine.

Whatever you want.

I know exactly what you mean.

It was a mix of yellow and green.

I kind of have things under control.

Now challenge your assumptions and write down as many alternatives as possible. It helps to put yourself into the mental shoes of someone you know well who has a very different worldview to yours.

What do you notice? Think about a recent client. What might you have taken for granted that could have opened a valuable space for exploration?

Using the here and now

A powerful way of helping clients get to know themselves better is to reflect back what is happening between you and the coachee in the here and now. This may mean pointing out the client's body language, summarising the way in which the two of you communicated just now, or drawing attention to a change in tonality or language in the client's narrative.

In the spirit of phenomenology, avoid making interpretations about what is happening, such as, "I notice you are sad". Instead, bracket your assumptions and describe what is happening – for example, "You're frowning", or, "I can see tears running down your cheeks." This helps the client to focus on the present moment and invites them to explore their ways of being in the world, the ways they react to others, how they communicate, what's important to them, the existence of certain beliefs and assumptions they might have, and the extent to which something might affect them.

Using the here and now best placed within, and indeed a crucial element of an authentic relationship. As Block writes:

> Authentic behaviour with a client means you put into words what you are experiencing with a client as you work. This is the most powerful thing you can do to have the leverage you are looking for and to build client commitment.
>
> (Block, 2000, p. 37)

It is tempting for coaches to jump ahead and offer tools or solutions, or to ask a powerful question in an attempt to unstick the client. However, the existential way is to ground the client in the present moment and so help them to explore their situation in depth and discover new ways of looking at a situation or event – particularly in relation to their worldview. Helping a client to form an understanding of this builds a strong foundation of who they are and what is important to them. This enables them to find their own solutions, make difficult decisions and take responsibility for their actions based on owning the choices they make.

Take a moment

Think about a recent coaching session of yours. Can you identify a situation where using the here and now could have been useful? In what way may it have influenced the remainder of the session?

Direct versus directive coaching

The existential coach appreciates the importance of a client deciding on their own plan of action and then taking responsibility for any consequences. They facilitate an exploration of the issue and help the client to come up with options in order to reach their goal. This is done in a non-leading, non-directive way.

The coach will not tell the client what to do, offer interpretations or wisdom, or direct them with any tools or step-by-step programmes that may have helped other people in similar situations. The coach acknowledges that no two situations or people are the same, and that every individual has to own their decisions if they are to accept responsibility and take charge of their life.

What the coach might do is invite the client to look at certain aspects that seem interesting or relevant with regard to what the client is talking about or trying to achieve. You might imagine this as sitting in the dark with a client, each of you holding a torch. The client always takes the lead and ultimately makes all the decisions. However, the coach may point their light at something that they perceive as relevant and potentially valuable, and may invite the client to explore it together.

The way that this is communicated is crucial, as you do not want the client to assume that this is something they have to look at just because their coach invites them to. It is essential that the relationship between coach and coachee is one of two fellow travellers, where neither has more power than the other.

While the coach may have advanced knowledge of human processes and motivation, she is not the expert. The client will always know more about themselves than anybody else in their lives. It is important to communicate this clearly so that an invitation, or pointing out something that seems interesting (contradicting statements or a change in facial expression), is not taken up as something that the expert recommends, and so that should be done, but rather something that can be rejected without any hard feelings on the coach's part. In fact, a client rejecting such invitations is a good indicator that they can make their own decisions and do not rely on others to guide them.

In this sense, the existential coach can be directional in that they might draw the client's attention to what they observe and invite them to go on a journey using an existential model of coaching. However, the client is always the captain of their ship, ultimately responsible for where they are going and the decisions they make.

Take a moment

Think about the last time you asked a leading question (a client or any other person). What was your agenda? What was the outcome?

What are you not telling me? Using the four worlds model in coaching

Above, you learnt about the four worlds model, which outlines the dimensions of how we experience being in the world (see Figure 4.1). This is not only a helpful model in which to understand the human condition, but can also help in developing a holistic picture of a client, and in identifying some of their blind spots.

For example, a client might tell you about their job tasks; their exercise routine and how important fitness is to them; their spiritual beliefs; their hopes for the future; and a fairly comprehensive account of their character and identity. You will therefore have heard a good deal about their physical, personal and spiritual worlds. At this point, you might point out that you have not heard the client talk about any significant relationship. Remember not to make the assumption that just because the client has not yet discussed this topic, it is not an important dimension for them; merely check in with them about whether or not it is significant.

Using the four worlds model (which we introduced above to outline the existential paradoxes of existence) is one way to create a holistic picture of a client in a practical way. When reflected back to the client, it can be used to initiate a process of exploration that helps them to build a strong foundation of who they are and how they experience being in the world.

Alternatively, if your approach to coaching operates in less depth, or focuses on specific areas of behaviour, you may choose to merely form a mental framework for your client; this can strengthen the relationship and open additional possibilities for interventions that are more likely to match the client's character and worldview. For example, if you have an understanding that your client values their relationships and social world very highly but puts little emphasis on their relationship with their body – showing little regard for health and exercise, for example – then this knowledge can help you choose an appropriate intervention.

Another way of looking at this model is from the top and envisioning it as a sphere with the spiritual dimension at the core of a human being and their physical dimension being the direct link to their surroundings (see Figure 4.2).

Developing a deeper appreciation for and understanding of your client as a whole (and hence, through the process of reflecting back and using the here and now, ultimately your client achieving this as well) can

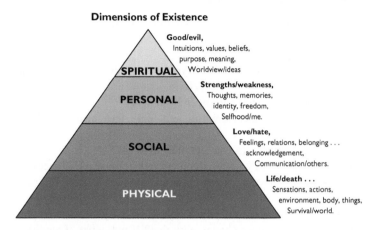

Figure 4.1 The four worlds of existence.
Source: adapted from van Deurzen (1997)

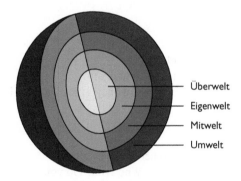

Figure 4.2 A sphere view of the four worlds model.

be pursued in a variety of ways. You may add to the whole as bits and pieces emerge from open conversation, or you may ask specific questions to explore each dimension in particular.

Hanaway and Reed (2014, pp. 225–227) outline a number of questions that may help us to explore each dimension, allow us to learn more about our client and, more importantly, allow our client to learn more about themselves and their way of being in the world. I have adapted their excellent foundation while adding to and amending it to some extent.

Umwelt/*physical dimension*

- How important is your current environment to you (your house, office, bedroom, flat share, etc.)?
- What does it provide you with?
- What would you lose or miss if you were elsewhere (e.g. moving house, changing jobs or office, etc.)?
- What is lacking in your current environment?
- What would your ideal environment look, feel, taste, smell and sound like?
- In what environment do you feel most ill at ease?
- To what extent does your environment reflect those preferences?
- What changes in your current environment would have the most benefit for you?
- How do you see yourself physically? How do you relate to your physical body? Are you happy with that? If not, what, if anything, are you doing in to change that?
- Where in the world do you feel most at home? What does being at home look like to you?

Mitwelt/*social dimension*

- How do you relate to other people?
- How comfortable are you with those around you?
- Do your keep your people close or are they spread across long distances?
- Are you in touch with people you grew up with? Do you make many new connections?
- How do you behave at parties or other social events?
  - Do you engage in conversation? Who with? Do you seek like-minded people or engage in debates and arguments? Do you tend to hang out with people you already know or are you find pleasure in getting to know new people?
  - Do you try to meet and greet as many people as possible or stick to a few longer conversations?
  - Are you there for the good food, the free drinks, the dancing and care less about the people?
- How important is the concept of "family" and your own family to you?
  - Are you close?
  - How often do you speak to them?

- o   What are the dynamics and relationships like between you and your family members?
- o   Do you need them to approve of your actions?
- Are you more comfortable leading or following?
- How do you describe your attitude towards conflict, disputes or arguments with other people?
- What are the most important aspects of your relationships with others?
- Which one/s is/are the most significant relationship/s in your life? Tell me about it!
- How do connections with others serve you in your life?
- What costs do you experience as a result of your relationships? How do they affect you?
- If you could choose to be friends with anybody in the world (assuming that they would reciprocate), who would you like to be friends with?
- Roughly how many people would you call besties/friends/colleagues/acquaintances/loose connection?
- Who are your enemies (if any)?

Eigenwelt/*psychological dimension*

- Who are you?
- How would you describe your personality or self-concept?
- What are your character strengths?[2]
- What is your most vivid memory (in relation to the topic of the coaching)? What is it about this event, object, person or experience that it remains so clearly in your thought?
- What's the most recurring thought that you hold in your mind?
- How do you relate to yourself?
- Are you meditating?
- What are the sort of thoughts and feelings that pass through your mind/body frequently? Have you noticed any patterns?

Überwelt/*spiritual dimension*

- What do you feel you couldn't live without?
- If you drew a spider diagram of what is important to you, what would you place at the centre?
- How would you want someone to finish this sentence if they were talking about you: "He was so passionate about . . ."?
- What are the beliefs which guide or govern your decision making and actions?

- What meaning do you find in your current position? How can that sense of meaning be increased?
- If you were to write your own epitaph, what would it say?
- What would you like your greatest gift to the world to be? What was your most meaningful achievement and why?
- If your heart had a voice, what would it stand for?

Take a moment

What other questions can you ask to explore each dimension? How could you phrase questions that are somewhat leading, categorical or closed in a more open manner as to free exploration and phenomenological inquiry? How would you capture the results of such a process (such as a mental map, or four quadrants on a flip chart or in a notebook)? You can practise this by watching a video of a coaching session or listening to somebody telling a story or talking about their life and then noting down elements in their narrative that correspond with the four dimensions.

Guidelines for existential practice

Peltier (2001, p. 161) pointed out existential philosophy's "enormous useful potential for the executive coach" and was the first to draft a set of practical guidelines as to outline what is important when practising in this way. He sets and elaborates on the following ten guidelines to consider (ibid., pp. 169–172), from which I shall quote only a sentence or two for clarification.

1 **Honor individuality** – First, approach each new coaching client with a freshness and willingness to see him or her as unique. Reinforce your client's points of view.
2 **Encourage choice** – Remind your clients that they choose their identity each moment of each day. Existence precedes essence. Their reputation need not constrain them.
3 **Get going** – The time for waiting is over. Exhort your clients to take risks, to get involved, to act, even to "live dangerously" sometimes.
4 **Anticipate anxiety and defensiveness** – Anyone who is a coaching client will experience anxiety. This is expected and "normal".

Beware of a client who reports no anxiety for he or she is not willing or able to notice or discuss feelings or their subjective inner state.

5 **Commit to something** – Existentialism urges us to get involved with the regular activities or everyday life, and to do it with a passion. Do not accept it when your clients hang back.[3] Urge them to get involved with those things that are important to them, even if others do not agree with their priorities.

6 **Value responsibility taking** – Existentialism urges us to take responsibility of the choices we have made. We did it, we chose it, and we now live with the choices and implication.

7 **Conflict and confrontation** – In the existential view, interpersonal conflict is unavoidable, yet many people characteristically avoid conflict. This is a mistake and coaches must assess their clients along this dimension.

8 **Create and sustain authentic relationships** – Both [coaches and clients] will benefit from authenticity in work relationship.[4] An authentic relationship occurs when both parties treat each other as autonomous entities to be respected. The truth is told and neither manipulates for personal benefit.

9 **Welcome and appreciate the absurd** – Organisations [just as life itself] are full of examples of absurdity, and anyone who has ever worked in a large (or small) organisation know how ridiculous things can get. This is simply normal. Assess your client to see how well they understand this fact and what they do with it.

10 **Clients must figure things out their own way** – No one can tell you the answers to the most important questions. You have to figure them out yourself, in your own way.

What clients can expect from an existential coach

Building on this framework, Hanaway (2018, pp. 103–104) adds the following 15 statements framed as expectations that a client seeking existential coaching may and should have in relation to the journey ahead:

1 They will be encouraged to speak up for themselves and the values they hold and will not be treated as if they fit into a pre-established model.

2 They will be invited into a creative dialogue where they take charge of their own exploration and are helped to think in new ways about making choices and decisions in their lives.

3   They will be helped to formulate with clarity who they think they are, where they are, where they want to go in their life.

4   They will be shown how to probe a little further and deeper and to challenge their assumptions about their lives, themselves, other people and the world they live in.

5   They will have an opportunity to tackle the conflicts in their lives and understand not only how they contribute to creating some of these but also how to face up to conflicts and surpass them, by learning about reciprocity, generosity and empathy.

6   They will be taught about dialectical principles and the way in which they make more of the paradoxes of human existence, using the ebb and flow of their lives to create movement for themselves.

7   They will be enabled to recognize their own ideology, in the form of their unspoken assumptions, their prejudice, their values, their most deep-seated beliefs and their predictive framework of human existence.

8   They will be taught new methods for tackling some of the distortions that have obscured their vision and they will increase their capacity for widening their perspective on their life.

9   They will be helped to take a broader and wider view of human existence in general and gain greater understanding of how life and the world actually work.

10   They will engage in debating their personal philosophy and will feel tested and challenged, but also helped to arrive at a more wholesome and complete view of the world.

11   They will abandon old destructive habits and replace them with new and more creative ways of proceeding in life, by reengaging with a meaningful purpose and project, which will make them feel passionate and enthusiastic about what they can contribute to the world.

12   They will examine their physical embodiment, and be helped to observe and note the habits that break them, so that they can break these habits instead.

13   They will become aware of the emotional and interactional patterns that create constant friction with other people around them and get better at resolving such conflicts or using the energy of those frictions to move on.

14   They will consider their self-image and their personal sense of who they are. They will become more able to become who they are capable of being and want to be.

15   They will improve their vision about the life they live, and the life they would like to live. They will do so by understanding first of all their own beliefs and values, but also by finding out more about human existence, its challenges, purpose and internal lawfulness.

I would add that it is important to be very aware of your own world-view, values and beliefs as a coach and any other contexts you may find yourself in. Who you are is intricately linked with the way that you practise, listen, ask questions, how your body responds and how your voice sounds when you answer a question or make a comment. We cannot *not* communicate and it is easy to guide, lead, push, suggest or otherwise influence a client in a particular direction. If these process are running underneath our awareness we do our clients a disservice. It is therefore crucial to nurture ongoing reflective practice. The most valuable way I know to do this is through regular coaching supervision sessions with a trained professional. That said, any form of reflection is better than remaining ignorant to the many dynamics that surround psychological work. I suggest to start with Hardingham (2004) to become more aware of your role as a coach and the skills and processes involved, followed by Bisson (2017) to develop a deeper understanding of what reflective practice entails. However, nothing that you do individually can replace the relationship and outside perspective that a supervision group or individual supervisor offer.

Reading through these guidelines, I assume that at times you will have felt some discomfort or unease (for example at the thought of having to "teach dialectical principles" or challenging the notion that conflicts can only be surpassed through "learning about generosity"). This is a sign that you already have or are developing an existential attitude as you find yourself questioning such guidelines, regardless of the reputation or experience of whoever brought them forward. It is important to note that every coach needs to find their own unique way of working with clients and that guidelines such as those outlined above (or anywhere else for that matter) can only ever act as mere suggestions, invitations or inspiration for your coaching work, for which you assume ultimate responsibility.

Take a moment

Review what has been mentioned in this book so far and the conclusions you made for yourself. How do these guidelines relate to your coaching practice? Which ones apply? Which ones do you aim to adopt in the future? Which ones might you disagree with and why? Should any be added? What can your clients expect from your coaching? I recommend an attempt at creating your own guidelines for existential(ly informed) practice and to write them down.

Models for existential coaching practice

Models are useful for showing the main workings of something in a simple form – a hypothetical description of a complex entity or process. It is arguably very difficult to fit something as complex as the existential approach to coaching into a neat model such as GROW[5] (Whitmore, 1992, 2017), PRACTICE[6] (Palmer, 2007) or TOOLKIT[7] (Bolton, 2017). Furthermore, it is important to distinguish between process model such as these, used during to manage a conversation and to understand the structure of it, and a model to grasp coaching as a whole and the elements involved in it (such as van Nieuwerburgh's model described in Chapter 2). Adding the fact that existentialism merely provides a framework for existential work allowing (and in fact encouraging) coaches to do it their own way and to challenge dogma and prescribed rules and processes, it is a difficult task to put forward a well-defined model for existential coaching.

The CREATE model

Hanaway and Reed (2014, p. 71) describe the CREATE model, illustrated in Figure 4.3. It is one possible interpretation of existential principles in a coaching framework and highlights the key steps of existential coaching, from making first contact to the ending of the coaching (but at the same time underlining the importance of elements such as the first contact and the significance of there being an end and the client's relationship with endings in this context, therefore encouraging the coach to pay extra attention to these key stages of the coaching process).

Contact starts before the first formal session at the time when coach and coachee become aware of each other. It is important to note that your client will usually be aware of your existence before meeting you or talking to you for the first time and will therefore have built up certain assumptions about you before you even know that they exist. Given that existential coaching is a meeting of worldviews, it is important to explore mutual assumptions and expectations about each other, and to include these in the first session, chemistry call or consultation.

The contract outlines each party's *responsibility* within the relationship. This responsibility is a central concern in existential practice and therefore make the contract somewhat more important than in other coaching approaches. It is almost inevitable that coach and client will re-contract throughout the coaching relationship as dynamics, goals, attitudes and other things keep changing. The existential coach will

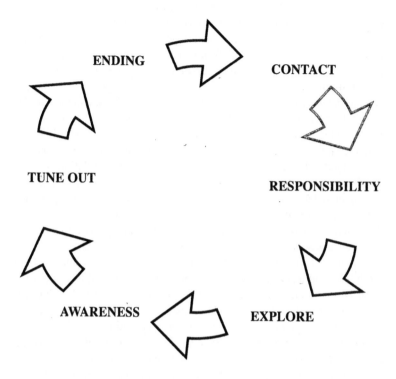

Figure 4.3 The CREATE model of existential coaching.
Source: Hanaway & Reed (2014)

emphasise that the client is ultimately responsible for the success of the coaching, which includes any of their actions as well as inactions. It is important to talk as clearly as possible about the degree to which you will be an active, influencing, encouraging, suggesting, challenging, exploring, facilitating or even advice-giving[8] part of the coaching process.

As described earlier, the main technique in existential coaching is phenomenological exploration. The coach is a fellow traveller who helps the client to *explore* what they choose to bring into the coaching space. This exploration, in conjunction with the core coaching skills (such as reflecting back, summarising, paraphrasing), will increase or instigate the client's (self-)awareness, which is the existential goal of coaching and ultimately allows the client to make more conscious choices and to take action based on what they uncover during their journey of exploration.

The coach aims to expand the client's *awareness* across all existential dimensions outlined in the four-world model (physical, social, psychological and spiritual). While during the exploration stage the coach's own opinions, values and beliefs are suspended (bracketing, tuning in), during the "tuning out" phase the coach can offer their perspective, any potentially helpful tools and techniques, and their experience of the client and the world. While tuning in, any coach would suspend themselves as much as possible and so this process may look similar across different styles. When *tuning out*, however, the individual style, identity, and speciality of the coach will shine through and each practitioner is encouraged to be authentic as possible. In the coaching relationship, the coach represents "the other" – the outside world – and it is important that the client is faced with this outside perspective in order to experience themselves in relation to others, as well as allowing them to benefit from the coach's expertise, which may be relevant and helpful (and indeed in many instances is the very reason a client seeks out a coach).

It is important to note that exploration, awareness and tuning out are rarely sequential steps. Coach and client may go back and forth between them until the client creates a meaningful way to deal with whatever they have brought into the coaching space. At this point, the coaching has reached an *ending*. It may also be that an ending will be reached simply because the resources for coaching have run out (perhaps the agreed number of sessions has been completed and no more funding is available). Endings highlight the existential themes of temporality and death (the death of coaching in this context); this can therefore also be an important topic to consider at the beginning of or during the coaching. When coach and client approach an ending (of a session or the relationship as a whole), it is an opportunity to check in with the client, which may uncover important dynamics in your client's relationship with endings in the context of the here and now.

The MOVER model

While CREATE is more clear about the *process* of existential coaching, the MOVER model (see Figure 4.4) emphasises the important *themes* when practising existentially, as well as how they are explored and worked with. Similarly to the CREATE model of existential coaching, I find this model particularly useful in that it is flexible in its possibilities for use and could indeed also be used to structure a conversation around these themes and hence depict a process as well as a reminder of the elements important to existential work.

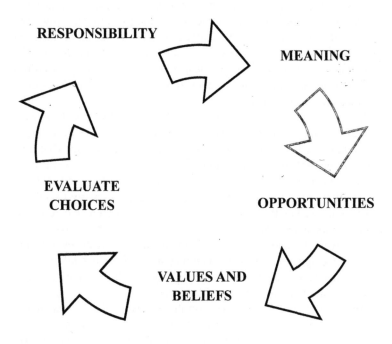

Figure 4.4 The MOVER model of existential coaching.
Source: Hanaway & Reed (2014)

MOVER places *meaning* in the position where people tend to look first when approaching a circular model such as this one (even though, as you will have noticed, there is no clear indication of a start or finish). Meaning is one of the main forces in human thinking, motivation and behaviour. The coach needs to understand the meaning that the client attaches to the coaching relationship and what they are looking for. Often, clients seek existential coaching because, on some dimension, meaning has been lost and their worldview has been challenged. Meaning, purpose and direction are central concerns that often run throughout the client's narrative; it is important for the coach to be able to listen to these concerns and reflect them back when they are related to the client's goals as to grow the client's awareness.

As we have learned, new awareness leads to new *possibilities*. But generally clients often seek coaching to create new *opportunities* and overcome obstacles. Existentially, obstacles also represent opportunities to live fully, to face life courageously, and to learn and grow. The existential coach explores the client's experience of facing obstacles in relation to their unique worldview and mode of being. Through reflective exploration, we help the client to identify or reframe these opportunities so that they can take creative action to overcome or sometimes even embrace their current obstacles.

It is therefore crucial to consider the client's *values and beliefs* (as well as the coach's) during existential coaching work as they are intricately linked with the client's map of meanings and hence what they regard as possible or unlikely pathways in their life. A way forward that is not aligned or congruent with one's beliefs and values (not authentic), is likely to fail or at least cost high amounts of energy to uphold. Existential coaches facilitate the client to arrive at authentic solutions to their problems by means of helping them discover themselves at this deeper level. Ultimately we aim to help the client to create an authentic mode of facing their existence on an ongoing basis, which allows them to become aware of available choices as they arise (rather than turning a blind eye out of comfort or to avoid anxiety).

An *evaluation* of these choices (in the context of their wider framework of existence taking into account their individual relationship with the existential dimensions) is therefore a crucial element and particularly important in coaching practice. During the coaching, the client is likely to produce various potential ways forward, and so will need to decide how to proceed and take action. Evaluating how these various options might influence the client's world and their relationship to him or herself offers valuable insight that opens up a space in which the best way forward (by the client's standards) can be chosen.

As outlined before, *responsibility* is one of the main tenets of existential thought; therefore, its importance should be highlighted throughout the coaching relationship, particularly when the client needs to choose a way forward and commit to it. Clients often look to the coach for answers or a particular tool or technique that will help them to identify the best way forward. While the coach might have the ability or knowledge to provide such help that would enable or inspire the client to create opportunities and find new understanding, coaching tends to be most powerful in the long-term when the client fully commits to the process as their own, takes responsibility for their course of action and in the process finds their own answers. This process is empowering and has long-lasting effects on the client's sense of self-efficacy and ability to approach and solve future challenges. It is often tempting for the coach to jump in and rescue a client from a difficult situation, particularly when we feel we know the answers (try to bracket them for the time being). However, it is important for the client to own their decisions and take responsibility for their actions or inactions, particularly in the context of which course of action they can commit to (and hence take responsibility for) in the context of what they came to coaching for achieve and the particular action plan they may have created in the course of the coaching session.

A conversation about the changes a client is planning to implement and questioning which choices and actions they are willing to take responsibility for often opens further discussion around meaning, which in turn leads to new opportunities and so on. The cycle continues.

Case studies for both models are offered in *Existential Coaching Skills: The Handbook* (Hanaway and Reed, 2014; Hanaway, 2018).

Notes

1 An invaluable skill to acquire in this regard is meditation, during which we train our mind to notice thoughts and feelings being evoked but without engaging with them.

2 Depending on your approach to coaching and your openness and ability to integrate tools and techniques from other approaches into an existential framework (see Chapter 7) there are a number of tools and techniques that may help your client gain some insight into some of these questions, in this case the Values in Action (VIA) strengths inventory available free via www.authentichappiness.com. However, keep in mind that a client's narrative is almost always richer than the results of a questionnaire, survey or psychometric test. That said, these tools can be a powerful way of unlocking or starting deep exploration of a client's existential dimension. It is crucially important in this process not to take the results (always a snapshot of the client at the time of completion) for granted, but instead to bracket their validity and start a conversation.

3 You can see how some existentialists urge their clients with a passion to get involved with life, while others may be more accepting of a client who chooses not to take action.

4 Keep in mind that Peltier (2001) writes in the context of executive coaching.

5 Goal – Reality – Options – Way forward.

6 Problem identification – Realistic, relevant goals developed – Alternative solutions generated – Consideration of consequences – Target most feasible solution(s) – Implementation of – Chosen solutions(s) – Evaluation.

7 Trust – Outcome – Open up – Loosen up – Know-how and resources – Identify tasks – Tidy up.

8 Given the nature of existential thought and particularly considering the guidelines to existential work (see Chapter 5) most existential coaches will not provide direct advice as they honour the client's individuality and appreciate that every client ultimately has to accept their own freedom and find their own solutions in their own way. However, as a coach you may have established

yourself as an expert in a particular field in which you now coach and you may have a strong mentoring background, for which clients seek you out. As I describe existentialism as fertile ground for integration, every coach can be informed by existential thought without following any particular guidelines or rules outlined in this book or any other.

References

Bisson, M. (2017). *Coach Yourself First: A Coach's Guide to Self-reflection.* Kibworth Beauchamp: Matador.

Block, P. (2000). *Flawless Consulting: A Guide to Getting Your Expertise Used.* San Francisco, CA: Jossey-Bass/Pfeiffer.

Bolton, N. (2017). Foundations. Unpublished manuscript. London: Animas Centre for Coaching.

Hanaway, M. (2018). *Existential Coaching Skills: The Handbook* (2nd edition). Guernsey: Corporate Harmony.

Hanaway, M., & Reed, J. (2014). *Existential Coaching Skills: The Handbook.* Guernsey: Corporate Harmony.

Hardingham, A. (2004). *The Coach's Coach: Personal Development for Personal Developers.* London: CIPD House.

Palmer, S. (2007). PRACTICE: A model suitable for coaching, counselling, psychotherapy and stress management. *The Coaching Psychologist, 3*(2), 71–77.

Peltier, B. (2001). The Existential Stance. In B. Peltier, *The Psychology of Executive Coaching: Theory and Application* (pp. 161–174). New York: Brunner-Routledge.

van Deurzen, E. (1997). *Everyday Mysteries.* London: Routledge.

Whitmore, J. (1992). *Coaching for Performance.* London: Nicholas Brealey.

Whitmore, J. (2017). *Coaching for Performance* (5th edition). London: Nicholas Brealey.

Chapter 5

Existential coaching in business

Why existential coaching is relevant to organisations

The term "existential" arguably doesn't enjoy the best press in the public eye. It is often portrayed as dark, deeply philosophical and concerned with questions that emerge for people in crisis. Therefore, it is not usually mentioned in the corporate world, even though many coaches, especially those working with executives, leaders and others in what I call "positions of great responsibility", are informed by existential ideas and report that their clients frequently bring existential questions and concerns into the coaching space.

From an existential perspective, life and business cannot be separated, and so the same anxieties and challenges emerge for clients of business coaching as they do for any other client seeking coaching, simply as they are also in the (business) world with others and are hence subject to the same givens. Peltier (2001) writes about this at length in *The Psychology of Executive Coaching*, which includes a chapter on existentialism. The difference seems to be that employees often do not deem it appropriate to consider these questions openly with their coach as the work is usually framed within performance and behaviour change. The existentially minded coach will see the profound connection between behaviour change, performance and a client's existential foundation and hence welcome and encourage conversations at this level. The other difference is that those at the top of organisations tend to be responsible for a larger number of people (as compared to, for example, the leader of a family, peer group or community meetup). Depending on the context within which the organisation exists, a leader's, manager's or executive's choice may affect hundreds, thousands or even millions[1] of people. The stakes are therefore arguably higher and the challenges at an existential level magnify accordingly.

It is true that three sessions of traditional coaching for performance will show clearer, more immediate results for the client than existential coaching, which are often much easier to measure and observe. However, the positive effects of performance coaching or behavioural work can be difficult to uphold in the long term without addressing the underlying causes of the client's initial challenges. Often new, similar habits and behaviours emerge until the underlying issues and relationships are addressed. Therefore, new understanding and shifts in thinking at an existential level, in combination with clear goal setting and some behavioural work, are likely to result in more sustainable outcomes that will benefit clients for years to come (rather than them needing to book another block of coaching sessions in a few months' time). Ultimately, this will save businesses money and create more authentic, motivated, resilient and confident workers that are less likely to avoid challenges and discomfort and that face difficult situations with courage and strength. In order to effectively work within a business setting a coach is therefore advised to develop an awareness of the wider spectrum in which human beings exist as to be able to choose their interventions appropriately and in the clients' best interest. This includes an awareness and understanding of the inherent interrelation between the client, others within the organisations and the wider context in which the organisation exists.

Existential leadership

Leaders are those in positions of great responsibility, typically at the top of a department, organisation or country (but may also lead a family, an afternoon book club or, arguably, their own lives). They are paramount to the success and culture of an organisation, and a lot of coaching work focuses on improving or optimising the performance (often characterised by the quality of their choices and the influence they have on the people they lead as well as the outside forces they shield the group from). A good leader has the interest of all stakeholders in mind and cares deeply about those stakeholders that they choose to attach the most meaning to (this may solely be the shareholders of the company but may also include the world at large – every leader is different). Leadership positions are often accompanied by above-average levels of pressure, stress and anxiety, and this is in part due to the fact that leaders are often seen and expected (including by themselves) to be "superhumans" (or "*Übermensch*" as Nietzsche called it). It can be easy to lose sight of a leader's humanness as they are often portrayed, or portray themselves as such in an effort to be become leaders in the first place.

However, leaders are first and foremost human beings, just like everybody else, and they are struggling with the same existential givens as all human beings are. Arguably they are more courageous (assuming that they have chosen to pursue the leadership position). It is noteworthy that in the recent past, an increasing number of leaders have started to appreciate that an authentic relationship with the people they lead results in a stronger connection with their people, often accompanied by higher levels of productivity and commitment across the organisation. The leader is a crucial factor in establishing a certain culture within the group and ultimately dependent on their group to do the work and create most of the solutions to problems.

Existentially, the same challenges and paradoxes are encountered regardless of whether one is leading one's own life or finds themselves employed to lead a Fortune 500 company or a country. That said, and as touched on earlier, leaders of people or organisations are often more vulnerable to certain existential issues than others due to the nature of their leading position, the weight of their responsibility, the complexity of relationships and the sheer magnitude of their task. In order to provide an overview of the themes and concerns involved from an existential perspective I have created a list of existential themes and their relevance to leaders including the role that coaching can play when working with such themes (see Table 5.1, adapted from Jacob, 2013).

When working with leaders existentially, it is important to note again that work and private life can rarely be separated. As outlined above, existential coaches approach the person as a whole, and so all facets of the leader's life matter, even when these are not brought into the coaching space by the client as a topic of conversation (think: "What are you not telling me?"). Furthermore, it is important to explore whether the leader *chose* to be in their leadership position or whether they were *thrown* into it.[2] This will have a profound impact on the client's sense of autonomy, the perceived pressure of the responsibility, how motivated and passionate they show up, and how they relate to themselves and others within and outside of the organisation.[3]

The role of existential coaching in leadership, then (compared to more behavioural or immediate performance- and results-oriented coaching), is to provide a trusted and safe place to pause; reflect; foster (self-) awareness; explore worldview and meanings; and provide support with regard to the challenging daily processes that such a role entails, thus facilitating authentic leadership. The existential coach notices when questions of meaning and authenticity enter the coaching dialogue, and they are able to work with these if the contract with the client allows for it.

Table 5.1 Existential themes in leadership, their relevance for those in managing positions and the role of coaching when working with such themes

Existential theme	Relevance to leaders	The role of coaching
Responsibility	Responsible for organisation's success, people's jobs, customers' needs or even health and wellbeing (depending on the organisation).	Accepting responsibility for choices. Exploring the boundaries of personal responsibility. Creating the foundation for authentic decision-making.
Choice	Needs to make important choices on a regular basis that potentially affect many people.	Becoming aware of choices and their link to values and worldview.
Freedom	Economic situation and resulting financial clamp-downs lead organisations to try and be as secure as possible → instead of making meaningful decisions or dealing with critical issues, senior staff are signing off minimal spending → loss of freedom.	Exploring organisational absurdity but also an awareness of ultimate freedom. Exploring options and consequences and creating conscious choices and acceptance of facticity.
Temporality	Job might not last, competitive environment, fast moving (business) world, cuts to resources, projects end, tasks end, people are being made redundant.	Explore attitude towards endings, help accept that it's a given.
Others	Expectations, competition, being watched and evaluated by "strangers", introducing change as part of the job, which people often reject. Being somewhat "above the herd" risks abandonment, rejection, judgement and difference.	Exploring the social world. How does the leader relate? Using the here and now/present relationship to explore relations with others. Becoming clear of one's role and others' worldview in relation to one's own.
Uncertainty	Economic instability. Successful leaders need to leap into uncertainty to maximise success and gain an edge on competitors; taking risks necessary to be successful. Yet, anxiety is considered a tabu in Western cultures.	Anxiety can be used. Practise staying alert to and mindful of the possibilities that uncertainty creates (new directions, different ways of engaging staff, welcoming input and collaboration, etc). Sitting with anxiety. Finding peace and strength in it.
Authenticity	Leader me versus at-home me, organisation's goals/values/worldview versus own goals/values/worldview.	Help noticing when s/he is stepping in and out of in/authentic state. Heightened awareness of self leads to more conscious choice, decision making and behaviours.

Meaning	Meaning is inter-relational, connected to what's going on across the leader's four worlds (no work-private separation). Questions leaders ask themselves: • What am I doing this for? • What am I bringing to this role, my team, the organisation? • Do I want to do this anymore and if so, then how do I do it in a way that means something to me? • What am I here for if not to lead? • What kind of leader do I want to be and what kind of meaning does that hold for me?	Help to differentiate between meaning *of* life and meaning *in* every task, activity, conversation etc, review, create and determine the two. Accept that they are ever-changing and need to be re-evaluated and re-created on an ongoing basis. Be open to change.
Organisational absurdity	Often a point is reached where nothing in the organisation seems to make sense anymore. And it often really doesn't. No consistency, in decisions, ridiculous rules, selfishness and greed etc. Leaders that try to make sense of it: suffer.	Accept that there are no ultimate grounds. Juggling absurdity of the organisation as a whole and meaning in projects in particular. Commitment is a choice, we make our own meaning.
Anxiety	Experiencing existential anxiety is inevitable. But leaders often try to block it for various reasons.	Embracing anxiety as a reminder to wake up and engage, to keep oneself at optimal engagement with life and open to one's reality → better judgement, more conscious choices through raised awareness, inspiring others and managing relationship better.
Conflict	Inner conflict (living up to demands or own standards). External conflict (see "others").	Using the here and now/present relationship to explore relations with others.
Bad faith	Leaders often deny that they are also human beings facing fear, doubt, anxiety, guilt, dread, unease, absurdity etc. They think they are or should be *Übermenschen* (supermen). Defence mechanism: keeping busy, inauthentic divide of self (can't bear silence, space or time to think).	Enlighten them to the struggles of life and allow them to experience some acceptance of these difficult feelings and emotions; learn to accept inevitability of inauthenticity and notice reasons for it (more conscious choice).

Source: adapted from Jacob (2013)

While you will recognise many existential themes when reading between the lines in literature on leadership, these themes are not often openly named as such. A few exceptions in particular relation to coaching are Jopling (2012), who writes specifically about coaching leaders existentially; LeBon and Arnaud (2012), who have developed a model of authentic decision coaching that is existential at heart; Hanaway and Reed (2014), who dedicated a section of their book to applying existential coaching to leadership and Hanaway (2018, 2019) who developed the latter into a book in its own right, being the first book-length publication on existential leadership.

Others who have written specifically about existential leadership include Agapitou & Bourantas (*Existential Intelligence and Strategic Leadership*, 2017), Boje (*Existential Leadership*, 2001), Lawler ("The essence of leadership? Existentialism and leadership", 2005) and Hermann (*Existentialism and Leadership Development*, 2011).

Furthermore, a number of inspiring books have been published relatively recently, informed by decades of working with leaders in the field or running highly successful business, highlighting existential themes in leadership and encouraging leaders to not just explore themselves in this light but also to present themselves authentically to their people. To coaches working with leaders I highly recommend the work of Brown (2012a, 2012b, 2013), Sinek (2011, 2014), Laloux (2014), Obolenski (2010), Hill (Hill, 2003; Hill & Lineback, 2011; Hill et al., 2014a, 2014b), D'Souza and Renner (2014), Friedman (2014), Goffee and Jones (2005) and Heifetz and Linsky (2002), to name only a few, with some more being mentioned in the resources section at the end of this book. All of these authors use an understanding of the human condition (and hence also the "leadership condition", if you will) to inform their writing and underline their ideas, theories, models and best-practice suggestions with ample examples grounded in the very real world of business and leadership.

Notes

1 The leader of a country or country-sized corporation (such as Apple, Amazon, Bayer or Johnson & Johnson) may indeed positively or negatively affect the wellbeing of large parts of the population with the choices that they make on daily basis.

2 It is quite common for those who become exceptionally good at a technical skill to be promoted into a position where they then need to manage people rather than processes. Not everybody is keen to work in this way but it tends to be the natural way up the corporate ladder and many of those who would

actually rather stay in their comfort zone or play to their technical strength feel it would be unwise to turn down the opportunity to step up their game (a decision often motivated by external drivers such as social standing, job title, perks or a significant pay rise).

3 Imposter syndrome has been on the rise in recent years, or rather an awareness that many employees who have been promoted into positions without their active choosing feel increasingly uneasy about their roles to an extent that it has been shown to cause a range of symptoms that affect their wellbeing and sense of authenticity.

References

Agapitou, V., & Bourantas, D. (2017). *Existential Intelligence and Strategic Leadership*. Lap Lambert Academic Publishing.

Boje, D.M. (2001). Existential leadership. Retrieved from https://business.nmsu.edu/~dboje/teaching/338/existential_leadership.htm

Brown, B. (2012a). *Daring Greatly: How the Courage to Be Vulnerable Transforms the Way We Live, Love, Parent, and Lead*. New York: Gotham Books.

Brown, B. (2012b). Leadership manifesto. In B. Brown, *Daring Greatly*. Retrieved from: https://brenebrown.com/wp-content/uploads/2013/09/DaringGreatly-LeadershipManifesto-8x10.pdf

Brown, B. (2013). *The Power of Vulnerability: Teachings of Authenticity, Connections and Courage*. Louisville, KY: Sounds True.

D'Souza, S., & Renner, D. (2014). *Not Knowing: The Art of Turning Uncertainty into Opportunity*. London: Lid Publishing.

Friedman, S.D. (2014). *Total Leadership: Be a Better Leader, Have a Richer Life*. Boston, MA: Harvard Business Publishing.

Goffee, R. & Jones, J. (2005). Managing authenticity: The paradox of great leadership. *Harvard Business Review, 85*, 86–94.

Hanaway, M., & Reed, J. (2014). *Existential Coaching Skills: The Handbook*. Guernsey: Corporate Harmony.

Hanaway, M. (2018). *Existential Leadership*. Guernsey: Corporate Harmony.

Hanaway, M. (2019). *The Existential Leader: An Authentic Leader For Our Uncertain Times*. Abingdon, UK: Routledge.

Heifetz, R.A., & Linsky, M. (2002). *Leadership on the Line: Staying Alive through the Dangers of Leading*. Boston, MA: Harvard Business School Press.

Herrmann, A.F. (2011). Existentialism and the development of leaders. Paper presented at the Central States Communication Association Convention, Milwaukee, WI, March. Retrieved from www.academia.edu/4070013/Existentialism_and_the_Development_of_Leaders

Hill, L.A. (2003). *Becoming a Manager: How New Managers Master the Challenges of Leadership* (2nd edition). Boston, MA: Harvard Business School Press.

Hill, L.A., & Lineback, K. (2011). *Being the Boss: The 3 Imperatives for Becoming a Great Leader*. Boston, MA: Harvard Business Review Press.

Hill, L.A., Brandeau, G., Truelove, E., & Lineback, K. (2014a). Collective genius. *Harvard Business Review*, *92*(6), 94–102.

Hill, L.A., Brandeau, G., Truelove, E., & Lineback, K. (2014b). *Collective Genius: The Art and Practice of Leading Innovation*. Boston, MA: Harvard Business Review Press.

Jacob, Y.U. (2013). Exploring boundaries of existential coaching. Master's thesis. Retrieved from www.academia.edu/8376861/Exploring_Boundaries_of_Existential_Coaching

Jopling, A. (2012). Coaching leaders from an existential perspective. In E. van Deurzen & M. Hanaway (ed.), *Existential Perspectives on Coaching*. Basingstoke, UK: Palgrave Macmillan.

Laloux, F. (2014). *Reinventing Organisations – A Guide to Creating Organisations Inspired by the Next Stage of Human Consciousness*. Brussels, Belgium: Nelson Parker.

Lawler, J. (2005). The essence of leadership? Existentialism and leadership. *Leadership*, *1*, 215–231.

LeBon, T., & Arnaud, D. (2012). Existential coaching and major life decisions. In E. van Deurzen & M. Hanaway (eds), *Existential Perspectives on Coaching*. Basingstoke, UK: Palgrave Macmillan.

Obolenski, N. (2010). *Complex Adaptive Leadership: Getting Chaos and Complexity to work*. London: Gower. Available online at www.gpmfirst.com/books/complex-adaptive-leadership

Peltier, B. (2001). *The Psychology of Executive Coaching: Theory and Application*. New York: Brunner-Routledge.

Sinek, S. (2011). *Start with Why: How Great Leaders Inspire Everyone to Take Action*. London: Penguin Books.

Sinek, S. (2014). *Leaders Eat Last: Why Some Teams Pull Together and Others Don't*. New York: Portfolio/Penguin.

Chapter 6

Ethical dimensions

Existential coaching as "therapy through the back door"?

Due to the nature of existential themes and the significance of the big questions in our lives, there are some risks to bringing them out in the open. In the course of an existential coaching session, given that the client has developed the necessary trust in their relationship with the coach, they may open up and start to think about areas of their life that they never dared to explore before, or hadn't been aware of. The existential coach may have initiated this exploration by making relevant connections between the client's narrative and its existential content; or they may have asked a specific question that tapped into the existential space, inviting the client to think more deeply about their presenting issue. This may allow painful or challenging memories and realisations to surface and the emotional space or existential void that could follow may be difficult to hold for an inexperienced or insufficiently trained practitioner.

Hence, offering clients a space to explore existential content bears some important ethical questions that every coach must ask themselves when choosing to work existentially. The ethically practising coach will be aware of the broader context of their work, the potential risks involved and will commit to ongoing reflective practice as to continue to ask themselves these important ethical questions rather than thinking that they can tick them off once at the beginning of the coaching relationship. While there can never be a complete list of such questions, I invite you to consider the following to get a feel for what is important to keep in mind and then build on them:

- Is the client willing and ready to explore (this specific area of) their life in more depth?
- Did I introduce the way I work to an extent that the client is able to make an informed decision whether to work with me or not? Has

anything changed in the way that we're working together or does anything need to change in order to deliver best practice? Does my client need to be aware of these changes in order to honour their informed commitment to the process? Have any new risks emerged along the way?

- Am I able to hold the emotional space that may be opened following the question I am about to ask?
- Am I aware of and have I communicated the limits/boundaries of my coaching? How far am I willing and able to go? How will I know when a client would be better off talking to a trained therapist?
- Can I recommend appropriate support if my client needs it (contacts for personally vetted therapists, counsellors, help lines, doctors, government services etc.)?
- How can I ensure my client is safe after they have left the coaching session?

It is important to note that most coaching sessions do not leave clients in a vulnerable state as to bear any real risk of harm. Coaching clients tend to be resourceful and well able to cope with their lives in general. And while some discomfort is inevitable when working existentially, most clients most of the time are resourceful enough to deal with these in a healthy way and use the feelings that have come up for productive reflection leading to growth.

However, sometimes a question asked by the coach or a seemingly simple reflection or summary may open up a space for deep exploration of the client's way of being in the world and they find themselves being faced with very uncomfortable or perhaps even horrifying truths about themselves or their life circumstances. While there is great value in challenging limiting beliefs or a worldview that you identified as an obstacle to the client's goal, this kind of challenge can at times destabilise the client's foundation of who they are and how they live their lives and in the process pull the metaphorical rug underneath their feet. In the immediate aftermath the world temporarily does not make sense anymore while you help the client build a new and even stronger worldview – a crucial element of profound psychological change. This process needs to be approached carefully. The existential coach must be most considerate as to how they work with a client, make sure that the client gives informed consent as to their way of working and is aware of the potential challenges of the journey ahead, of both the possibilities as well as the risk that accompany an existential exploration.

It is crucial that the existential coach is fully aware of their level of training and ability to hold the coaching space and ensure their client's safety and wellbeing. You do not want to open Pandora's box only to find that you will need to send your client home feeling vulnerable and fragile. As a coach (any coach, but particularly as an existential one) you have a responsibility to establish reflective practice (e.g. through regular supervision), to know your limits and to find the courage to stop working with a client when you feel they would be better off working with somebody else.

Existentialism as fertile ground for integration of other approaches

One of the cornerstones of existential philosophy is that people make their own rules and that, as long as we take responsibility for our choices, we are not bound to any universal laws of what we can or can't do. Therefore, as mentioned before, there is no unified school of existentialism and many thinkers disagree on many issues beyond the core themes. It is in this light that existentialism provides fertile ground for the integration of many other approaches to coaching practice, along with their specific tools, methods and techniques.

While existentially minded coaches will aim to form a holistic picture of the client and use the phenomenological mode of inquiry into what they are bringing into the coaching room, this often happens in the background. Furthermore, the specific context of the coaching might deem it inappropriate to go into depth or reflect back to the client any relevant connections with regard to their way of being in this world. Particularly in time-limited professional contexts, existential themes might not be discussed openly; however, they can still help the coach to grasp their client's experience.

For example, questions of meaning might be the obstacles to growth. However, rather than asking specifically about what provides meaning for a client in their life, the coach might read between the lines in the client's narrative to extract this information, slowly building a coherent picture of the client until it might be relevant to reflect it back.

Until it does become relevant to introduce existential themes into the session, they might simply inform the coach's understanding of the client as a person. Big questions of life might not be at the forefront of the discussion. As such, any coach might work with themes of responsibility, meaning and how a client relates to others and the world, but in their own style and approach. In this regard, the coach is free to develop their own existential understanding of the world, letting their practice be guided by their personal and professional background and training, their individual skillset, and their unique view on human behaviour, motivation and wellbeing. The statement "who you are is how you coach" is more relevant to the existential approach to coaching than to any other.

The interested reader may refer to an article I wrote around the notion of therapy through the backdoor (Jacob, 2011), my chapter on integrating coaching and therapy from an existential perspective (Jacob, 2013) and a recent piece of research into Master Certified Coaches' perception of the boundaries of coaching (Sime & Jacob, 2018).

References

Jacob, Y.U. (2011). Therapy through the back-door: The call for integrative approaches to one-to-one talking practices and Existential Coaching as a possible framework. Unpublished manuscript. Retrieved from www.coachingandmediation.net/downloads/01%20-%20Research%20&%20Publications/2011-Jacob-Therapy_Through_the_Back_Door.pdf

Jacob, Y.U. (2013). An existential perspective on the integration of coaching and therapy. In N. Popovic & D. Jinks (eds), *Personal Consultancy* (pp. 271–291). London: Routledge.

Sime, C., & Jacob, Y.U. (2018). Crossing the line? A qualitative exploration of ICF master certified coaches' perception of roles, borders and boundaries. *International Coaching Psychology Review, 13*(2), 46–61.

Chapter 7

Establishing an existential coaching practice

The challenge of selling coaching services

Psychotherapy has a long history and is an established field of practice with a clear target group: people in severe distress. Existential psychotherapy and counselling as a branch of this field also goes back some time and hence clients who are seeking help generally know when the time has come to do so and where to look. Coaching, in comparison, has emerged only very recently and despite its boom in popularity in the past decade I see many qualified coaches struggle to sign up new clients.

One reason for this is that coaching clients, as mentioned above, tend to be quite resourceful and able to deal with their life relatively well. Coaching is often depicted as helping people move from *okay* to *good*, or from *good* to *amazing*, which means that there isn't necessarily a problem that needs fixing. Combined with the fact that most people tend to spend money only when something is broken rather than to invest during a time of relative stability in order to grow, build resilience and strengthen their core as to prepare for future adversity or to generally improve the quality of their lives, makes coaching a harder sell. I believe this is why many coaches, particularly in a corporate setting, still offer packages aimed at problem-solving and conflict resolution rather than growth and development (or at least they frame their offer in this way when they market their services).

People tend to invest resources (time, money, energy, etc.) for one of two reasons: (1) to avoid or move away from something that pains them, or (2) to gain or move towards something they desire. Considering the above outlined spending habits of your potential clients and due to the fact that coaching and attracting client are two very different skill sets (with the latter in my experience being somewhere between under-developed and non-existent for the majority of coaches) as well as considering the lack of mention this topic receives in the academic literature, I would like to outline a few basic strategies that can help an aspiring coach to take their first steps into creating a steady stream of clients and assist already established coaches to learn how the existential niche may provide a unique selling point to their business as well as open up new avenues for marketing and promotion.

Since building a flourishing coaching business works in similar ways regardless of the specific approach, I will offer some general pathways to attracting clients but always with a specific focus on the existential coaching niche. Since my background is not in marketing or sales but having been thrown into a position where I needed to develop my entrepreneurial skills and mindset,[1] the techniques and suggestions presented here are in no way meant to be comprehensive but, in line with the introductory nature of this book, shall act as a mere starting point for further exploration. I will be echoing what I've learned from Animas's founder and one of my favourite entrepreneurs in the field of coaching, Nick Bolton, as well as ideas and strategies from Chandler and Litvin (2013), Vaynerchuk (2018), Hayden (2013), Brown-Volkman (2003), Cornelius (2013), Cardone (2012), Ries and Trout (1994, 2001), and Godin (2005).

In the face of the overwhelming amount of available material on marketing, branding and sales I wanted to make an effort to suggest a few sources that have helped me understand the landscape better, position myself as an existential coach and attract enough clients to hone my sales skills in an ethical and authentic way with the client's best interest always at the forefront of my decision making.

Take a moment

Drawing on your current level of knowledge and experience, brainstorm as many ways as you can that may help you find clients for your (existential) coaching practice.

The crucial importance of the relationship – part II

Now before we get started, I want to share something I have learned along the way: People don't buy products and services – People buy people.

What I mean by that is that as long as your coaching is not actively in the way of someone's development, your clients will find value in it. Often it is enough simply to show up and to listen for your client to get some amazing results. Any additional coaching skills you can provide will add to the experience and value of the relationship. But if you get the relationship right then you are already half way there. McKenna and Davis (2009) suggest that 30 per cent of the success in coaching can be attributed to the relationship between coach and client, and with 40 per cent being attributed to external factors beyond your control, you are literally half-way there. Client's expectations, they suggest, make up 15 per cent of the success pie, which means that if you get your branding right and create the right environment, then this accounts for another quarter of the success that you can influence. This means that only 15 per cent can be accredited to the particular coaching approach, your coaching skills and the questions you ask, the way you listen and your theoretical underpinning.

While McKenna and Davis's (2009) work is based on thousands of studies and many meta-analyses into the success of psychotherapy (Asay & Lambert, 1999; Lambert & Barley, 2002) and considering that existential coaching is arguably a lot closer to this area than other approaches to coaching, it would be preposterous to claim that the numbers are as clear cut as they seem on paper. Nevertheless, it demonstrates an important trend, which is that the relationship is the most important factor in the equation. Therefore a coach who can create a good relationship (as in a working alliance) with a client has a twice as valuable skill than a coach with good coaching skills.

If we now consider the relationship from a sales angle, those who have a good connection with a prospect (someone interested in your service or product) are much more likely to buy into your coaching. And since they already have a good relationship with you they will also expect a lot more results, which due to the 15 per cent attributed to hope and placebo means that it is very likely that they will actually get more out of the coaching before you have even started. That is the reason why many coaches invest a lot of energy and resources into building their personal brand, networking, visibility and reputation. And while it is true that many salespeople out there are making false promises based on a fabricated personas and polished personalities and lifestyles, as a coach you do not simply sell and then go your separate ways again. The sale is only the beginning of the real relationship you're selling. And this is doomed to fail unless you are being authentic and genuine. The more authentically you put yourself out there, the more successful you will be in making genuine connections and to form relationships with potential clients.

Once you have learned or allowed yourself to connect to others in this way, you have mastered the most important step. The rest is a process of learning how to talk about what it is you offer and to position your services in a way that a prospect is able to see that coaching will you is more valuable to them than holding on to the money that you are charging. But let's start with the basics and consider some ideas how you could start building those relationships.

How to get clients

Now, consider the following list of ways of finding new clients:

- Word of mouth from existing clients.
- Word of mouth from friends, non-coaching colleagues and associates, acquaintances, etc.
- Referrals from other practitioners (coaches with different specialities, therapists, counsellors, mentors, consultants).
- Other strategic partners (e.g. organisations, institutions, wellness centres, schools etc.).
- Local meet-ups, networking groups or regular community gatherings.
- Web-based training (webinars or open online courses).
- Face-to-face workshops.
- Public speaking.
- Writing (books, ebooks, articles, blogs, journals, magazines, newspapers).
- Marketing-aware web-presence (being vocal about your job, passion, special offers and daily experiences as a coach on social media and other online platforms – as appropriate).
- Local offline advertising (flyers, posters, noticeboards, newspapers, direct mail).
- Web-based advertising (targeted Google or social media ads).
- Guerrilla marketing and other creative approaches.
- Email marketing (building a mailing list).
- Creating your own community (local or global, from running a highly engaged Facebook group or local meetup to becoming a thought leader in your niche).

Which of these methods are you already using? Why do they work for you? Which ones are you not using and why? I invite you to question and explore these reasons in depth. While your reasoning may be solid and grounded in facts, when I work with coaches on building or expanding their businesses I often find that existential themes such as uncertainty, freedom, responsibility, lack of courage, not having identified a clear why (based on values, beliefs and worldview) or not knowing who you are trying to attract sit at the root of holding back from going out there and giving it a go.

Take a moment

Which of these strategies do you see working particularly well with an existential approach? Which ones might be problematic?

Referrals

A powerful way to create a flow of clients as an existential coach is to build a strong network of strategic partners who work with clients who could benefit from an existential exploration as to complement, follow-up from or preceding the work that they are offering. Building these relationships is likely to be work-intensive and may take considerable time, effort and energy, yet in the long term it tends to create the most stable flow of clients (depending on how well you choose the partner).

In existential coaching, you might expect referring partners to be therapists and counsellors whose clients are now able to cope with life and have overcome acute crises in their lives but would like to keep working with a trained professional who does not shy away from big questions. Partners might also be other coaches who have reached the limit of their niche (e.g. behavioural coaching, time management etc) or who choose not to work with deeper issues or who generally feel they have exhausted their repertoire and identified a need in their client to address some bigger underlying themes in their lives – in other words professionals who work with people on specific life issues rather than life itself. They may also include schools, wellbeing departments of Universities, individual teachers, healers, mentors, consultants, organisational psychologists, local councils or other larger institutions. Referral fees are not uncommon (this may go both ways) and need to be negotiated individually and depend on a complex set of factors that would go beyond the scope of this section.

As an exercise, identify as many potential strategic partners as you can. For each of them, state in some details how your existential work may complement, contribute or represent the ideal follow-up to the services that they offer. You may need to do some research on their target audience and the process in which they work. The best way to do this (while at the same time starting to build a relationship) is to talk to them in person. Make sure that you don't come across as looking only for your own benefit. Good strategic partners benefit each other in similar ways (either through mutual referrals or via referral fees). At this early stage, simply be interested in and curious about their work, with a potential option of doing some mutually beneficial work together (try to tell them about it at the end of the conversation or at a second meeting so that you can plan how to position your services in line with their offerings.

A shorter-term, yet far simpler pathway to referrals is to list as many people as you can think of who may know somebody that could potentially benefit from existential coaching. These may be friends, non-coaching colleagues and associates, acquaintances or people that you have heard people talk about and who you could ask to make an introduction. Approaching those who already know you (or know you by association) asking for help in promoting a good cause (this may range from simply helping you out or doing you a favour, all the way to changing the world for the better "one client at a time" as you follow your life's mission to help people live more courageous and fulfilled lives. Obviously the way you approach this depends on your personal values, your *why*, and what you are passionate about. Remember that in order to build authentic, strong and fruitful relationships, presenting your *why* has to be genuine and believable and hence needs to be presented with passion and in a way that whoever you talk to can relate to on an emotional (and ideally a value-based) level. Those who share your beliefs and values and are keen to support your long-term goals are most likely to help you. I recommend Sinek's (2011) *Start with Why* (you may start with his TED Talk) and George's (2015) *Finding your True North*. Both books are themed around leadership, however, their principles apply to anybody, regardless of whether you are the head of department, head of a country or head of your own body.

The narrower the audience that you are trying to reach, the more effective you can plan your marketing and position what you are offering in the framework that you target group will most likely connect to. However, given the fact that existential issues affect anybody alive and in the world with others, the potential target group for whom existential work could be helpful is overwhelming. I suggest to start by picking a group of people that you can see the most benefit in working with (by your own standards – this could be a particular industry you'd like to support, their ability to pay high fees, a particular need for existential work, the fact that you have easy access to them, etc.). Think about who might know people open to engage in coaching (and hence, depending on the way that you choose to work, likely to invest in their personal, professional and spiritual development before the emergence of a major crisis, people who aim to build resilience and defences or those with a curiosity for better understanding life in general and their personal philosophy in particular. You may refer back to Hanaway's (2018) list of client expectations to help you and your referral contacts identify potential clients. As you can imagine this list may go into the hundreds and I encourage you not to shy away from the task ahead. Referrals are the most powerful way to get in front of potential clients and, due to the trust-by -association make it most likely that clients sign up for a chemistry call, introduction session or coaching package.

Groups, workshops and public speaking

Clients are more likely to approach you for coaching when there is already a relationship. That is the reason why "warm" referrals or introduction through a mutual contact work better than "cold" advertising approaches. Research has shown that this holds true even if the person recommending a service or product is a stranger. That is why testimonials work. Realistically you will most likely not be the best coach in the world (by definition there can only be one) and it is very likely that there will be other coaches within in your area of expertise who will have had better training or more experience, fancier websites or more competitive prices. However, time and again clients choose coaches that they already are or feel connected to in some way as there is a baseline level of trust. The stronger the relationship or connection, the more of an advantage you will have against your competition and the higher the chances that a client asks you for a consultation. Trust can also be built through credentials (e.g. a book to your name, accreditation by a respected coaching body, relevant education/training, media presence or having established yourself as an expert in some other way), but there will always be more uncertainty for clients when approaching somebody they've never met in person than to talk to somebody they already have spent some time with.

Hence, an excellent way to form new relationships and get to know potential clients (or strategic partners) is at events. These can be network events especially set up to bring people together for professional reasons, but any other group that brings people together (ideally face to face) and allows people to get to know you, to get a sense for who you are and how you are being, the way you talk, your demeanour, body language, vibe and energy. If they have already spend some time with you, and then find out through conversation that you are passionate about coaching and helping people navigate their human condition, it is much less of a courageous step to show curiosity for your services. Likewise, it is much easier to ask them whether they know somebody (including themselves) who might be interested in such services. The art in this process is to learn how to build trust and rapport in a relationship and to identify an appropriate time to steer the conversation in this direction or use the right cue to position your services within the natural flow of the conversation.

Adding the element of positioning yourself as an expert, running (free or paid for) workshops, lectures, talks or presentations in your community or network will allow you to share some of the main messages from your work, show your passion and knowledge about the subject area and make it easy for attendees to connect with you during or after such events. Even a podcast, interview, blogpost, being strategically active on social media (and vocal about what you are passionate about) as well as any other form of getting yourself out there to a broader audience (even if your audience is not directly in the room with you) will build a (one-way) relationship between your listener/reader/viewer and yourself and hence make it more likely that they might reach out to learn more about your service.

Make sure that you create time to connect during or after any activity that you run and encourage people to start a conversation with you. Any form of contact will make it more likely that someone takes the next step and the longer you are in contact with someone the stronger the relationship will grow. Be aware that a particular set of skills is required for organising such events and creating opportunities to be put into the spotlight, for creating a loyal followership on social media or via a mailing list, or to positioning yourself as a thought leader or expert in a particular niche. Again, this book is not intended to provide a comprehensive guide, but the main message here is to educate yourself about these techniques, to be courageous when putting yourself out there and to believe in the value of the service you provide. Remember that it does not have to be the best service, it just has to be good enough and available right now in order to provide value for your client. You do not need to pretend you are the best or most suitable (unless that's a genuine belief). Often it is enough to simply be there and to have formed a relationship. If you think about it, many romantic partnership are formed in the same way.

Take a moment

Brainstorm a number of community groups that you would enjoy getting involved in as well as local network events, conferences, or meetups that you could join. Have a think about what kind of topics you know more about than the majority of the others within that group (if you are really into something, chances are you know more about it than most people). And this does not even have to be coaching related. In my experience, anything that people do or care about is in some way related to existential themes, so you can always make a link to your coaching work.

Advertising

Advertising works best if you have gone through the motions of thinking deeply about your business, having identified your unique selling point, key outcomes you are offering or problems that you are offering solutions to, you know who your target group is and you have some budget to invest into the process. While some forms of advertising are free and there are many creative ways to market your services at low or no cost, in the vast majority of cases you will have to pay for advertising space. Depending on your price structure, you may get a return on such an investment eventually and this is the goal of a successfully set up advertising campaign. Once you find a way that works for your business (such as google ads if you have a professional website designed to convert clients, Facebook ads if you target an audience that share common interests, groups or geographical locations or ad placements in your local café, newspaper, a trade magazine or even via direct mail or flyers), it can create a steady flow of prospects reaching out for consultations. However, the process of finding the right strategy can be pricey and your ads really need to hit into the heart of what your target audience desires or is trying to avoid, respectively. I recommend to experiment in small increments and keep a record of what worked and then to steadily adjust your strategy. Working with a business coach, marketing or branding consultant can be invaluable in this respect, though, as most coaching, it is not a prerequisite for success but likely to speed up the process considerably.

A note on niching

A message that you will have heard many times is that you need to find your niche. Many coaches (a younger version of myself included) seem to understand this as having to define in as much detail as possible who your ideal clients are (hint: my marketing consultant advised me that it is often a version of yourself with similar characteristics, values, beliefs, interests and experiences and I have seen this trend hold true across many practitioners[2]). Defining aspects may include their age, geographical location, job title, industry, worldview, language they use, shopping preferences, group affiliations, browser history and the list goes on. The narrower the audience is defined that you are trying to reach, the more directly you can target them as to align your messages and speak to their specific problems and desires.

A niche, however, beyond the people that your service is for, can also be the particular problem that you are solving (e.g. existential crisis prevention, getting unstuck in your career or filling a feeling of emptiness in life) or the outcomes you create (existential resilience, living courageously or keeping it real), the service, process or experience that you are providing (existential coaching is still a very small niche), or simply you as an person (by definition there is nobody out there just like you and the more different you are the more you will stick out as a coach[3]).

Take a moment

What other ways of attracting clients can you think of? Where else could you learn more? Who are your role models in the coaching industry or with regards to successful entrepreneurship? Who else could you talk to in order to get inspiration for your own approach to getting more clients?

There are of course many ways to run a successful business and the above can only scratch the surface of what is possible. Nevertheless, I hope that I was able to equip you with a few techniques, methods and ideas that will attract some clients to your developing existential coaching service and that the sources I mentioned at the beginning of this chapter will be a good starting point for acquiring the skill set necessary to build a flourishing existential coaching practice. I appreciate that this skill set is quite different to what is needed in order to be a good coach (and some of them might even seem counter-intuitive). However, I believe it is important for coaches to learn how to market themselves in an authentic, honest and genuine way as to create true win–win outcomes for their clients. I know first-hand as well as through hundreds of clients, coaches, students and supervisees, that the value we provide often surpasses clients' expectations many times over and if were to compare the fees we charge against the benefits that often stay for a lifetime, the coach almost always gets the shorter end of the bargain. But money aside, the sheer joy of facilitating such positive and generative effects on your clients and, in turn, the people around them, is a cause worth pursuing and this realisation certainly shifted my mindset in that now feel obliged to offer what I've learned over the past decade to the wider community. I truly believe that if more people were to adopt an existential understanding of the world and themselves, chose to face their givens, explore what they believe in, embrace the human condition as the stuff that makes life worth living and chose courageously, then the world would be a better place, or at least we would get more out of the experience and spend less time distracting ourselves from living. Hence, if I hear somebody express curiosity about philosophical questions, a desire to better understand the world and people's behaviour (including their own) or a dilemma that seems to be linked to an existential theme, I feel I would do them a disservice not to mention that there is help out there (and perhaps even with me if that's appropriate in the context of the encounter).

Notes

1 I entered coaching out of a passion for the process and a desire to help people live better rather than building a business and wish somebody would have pointed out to me at an early stage in my training that if I wanted to be a coach I would necessarily have to become an entrepreneur. I now make this clear to my students from the outset of their training as it pains me to see the vast number of great coaches who end up working with very clients or give up on formally coaching clients altogether due to the frustration of struggling with finding new clients

2 While I work with people across the spectrum of characters and job titles, I have realised that those whom I seem to attract the easiest are often quite similar to me in many respects and I enjoy the work tremendously. It also makes it easy to market to this target group as you can simply speak from the heart in your marketing. We are attracted by what is similar to us and hence a bond is formed quickly when we share our values and beliefs, which strengthens the relationship. However, it is a tricky situation as we are prone to making assumptions based on our own experience and I recommend regular supervision and careful ongoing reflection if you choose to pursue this course of marketing.

3 For years I had been hiding that I am passionate about longboarding (a form of skating) from my professional network. I was afraid that that I would be judged based on the stereotypes that people may have around skateboarding. When one day, a few days after a network event that I would have missed if I hadn't skated there, the organiser wrote a blogpost about

personal branding mentioning a "skateboarding coach" that she will never forget, I decided to stop hiding aspects of my personality that others may find strange. Seth Godin's Purple Cow principle and Gary Vaynerchuk's rise to success are great resources in this respect.

References

Asay, T.P., & Lambert, M.J. (1999). The empirical case for the common factors in therapy: Quantitative findings. In M. A. Hubble, B. L. Duncan & S. D. Miller (eds), *The Heart and Soul of Change: What Works in Therapy*. Washington, DC: American Psychological Association.

Brown-Volkman, D. (2003). *Four Steps to Building a Profitable Coaching Practice: A Complete Marketing Resource Guide for Coaches*. Lincoln, NE: iUniverse.

Cardone, G. (2012). *Sell or Be Sold: How to Get your Way in Business and in Life*. Austin, TX: Greenleaf Book Group Press. [I recommend the audio book, and to be aware that he is going to try and sell you more of his services and products while reading.]

Chandler, S., & Litvin, S. (2013). *The Prosperous Coach*. Anna Maria, FL: Maurice Basset.

Cornelius, C. (2013). *One in Ten: How to Survive your First Ten Years in Business*. Compton: Appletree Publications.

George, B. (2015). *Finding your True North*. Hoboken, NJ: John Wiley & Sons.

Godin, S. (2005). *Purple Cow: Transform your Business by Being Remarkable*. London: Penguin Books.

Hanaway, M. (2018). *Existential Coaching Skills: The Handbook* (2nd edition). Guernsey: Corporate Harmony.

Hayden, C.J. (2013). *Get Clients Now! A 28-Day Marketing Program for Professionals, Consultants, and Coaches*. New York: Amacom.

Lambert, M.J. & Barley, D.E. (2002). Research summary on the therapeutic relationship and psychotherapy outcome. In J. C. Norcross (ed.), *Psychotherapy Relationships that Work: Therapist Contributions and Responsiveness of Patients*. New York: Oxford University Press.

McKenna, D., & Davis, S.L. (2009). Hidden in plain sight: The Active Ingredients of Executive Coaching. *Industrial and Organizational Psychology*, *2*, 244–260.

Ries, A., & Trout, J. (1994). *The 22 Immutable Laws of Marketing*. New York: HarperBusiness.

Ries, A., & Trout, J. (2001). *Positioning: The Battle for Your Mind*. New York: McGraw-Hill.

Sinek, S. (2011). *Start with Why: How Great Leaders Inspire Everyone to Take Action*. London: Penguin Books.

Vaynerchuk, G. (2018). *Crushing It! How Great Entrepreneurs Build their Business and Influence – and How You Can, Too*. New York: Harper Business.

Summary

It goes without saying that a short coaching book about existential philosophy can only scratch the surface of a subject area of such magnitude and complexity. However, I hope I was able to open some doors of perception so that you were able to intellectually grasp as well as personally experience the basic tenets of the human condition (by relating theory to some specific life situations or through some of the exercises) as outlined by the existential thinkers mentioned in this book.

If you are an experienced coach I hope you will be or have been able to take some its content into your coaching room and, whether implicitly or explicitly, add value to your work and ultimately to your clients' lives through the theories, concepts, tools and techniques that I presented. If you are new to coaching perhaps I was able to spark your interest sufficiently as to explore further training in this exciting new field of practice. I found that providing a space for people (coaches, clients or otherwise) to grapple with existential questions is one of the most challenging, yet also most rewarding activities that I can think of and I feel blessed each day for being able to make a living from it. Looking at specific content through an existential lens almost always opens up new possibilities and produces longer lasting and more meaningful change.

Regardless of your coaching experience, I believe that we live a richer life when we allow ourselves to come face to face with our human condition, develop the courage to sit with it for some time, to look into the abyss and to consider some of the big questions despite the eerie feeling of anxiety that goes with such an exploration. I therefore hope that this book will have offered a tangible and desirable alternative to chasing comfort and in turn will help you to make more courageous decision in your life going forward, whether that is professionally as a coach or generally as a human being.

I furthermore wish that I was able to provide a sufficiently positive perspective on our human condition in general and the existential givens in particular as to encourage you to not just manage and accept, but to embrace the entire spectrum of your existence. Rethinking our concept of happiness away from experiencing comfort, safety and positive emotions and towards including life's more challenging experiences in a meaningful way will allow us to actually achieve a state that we could call lasting happiness.

When clients enter the coaching room they tend to ultimately look for some form of feeling good or better about themselves or about the world, regardless of their presenting goal or problem. It was my aim to demonstrate how these goals are necessarily connected to how a person experiences themselves at each of their existential dimension so that an insight in the complex relations of the person can either become part of the conversation or at least help the coach to appreciate their clients at a deeper level as to be able to show more empathy, connect more authentically and help them to make more courageous and rewarding decisions in their lives.

Lastly I hope that I made it clear that every coach will practice in their own unique way and that there is no one best way of doing existential coaching. It rather is a way of being with clients and helping them explore whatever they bring into the coaching space with some shared underlying assumptions about the human condition. Within the framework of existentialism you are (condemned to be) free to do your own thing. This is not only encouraged, but inevitable. I see too many coaches trying to follow an established play book and apply set and "proven" processes to successful practice. While it is helpful at the beginning of your professional journey (and in fact I would encourage the novice coach to experiment with as many processes as possible), I believe that we can only truly connect as human beings (and thereby unleash the real power of the coaching relationship), when we learn to *be* with somebody first (authentically, genuinely and unapologetically human) before we introduce the many possible ways of *doing* coaching into the mix. An understanding of the human condition lies at the heart of such an endeavour.

On a practical level, having drawn meaningful lines between existential coaching as you understand it and other approaches, having thought about how you can integrate it into your existing coaching style, and having filled our tool box with a few new existential gems, you now have the knowledge to let existential philosophy inform your practice and your way of being with your clients. From here, it's all about practice! And that means being courageous and getting yourself out there. I hope that those new to coaching were able to get the ball rolling via some of the business advice provided in the last chapter, and that the more experienced among you will have gathered some helpful new ideas. I would like to encourage coaches of all levels of success and experience to keep one or two practice clients willing to let you try out some new stuff (contract this carefully as to practice ethically). There is no shame in continuous professional development in a real life setting. On the contrary, it communicates your willingness to learn and develop, is a brilliant opportunity to promote a "pilot programme at a special discount" and allows a coach to leave the safe haven of practice-as-usual and charter into the unknown sea in an ethical way (with informed consent from the client to experiment). More often than not the coaches that underwent my training courses have found new islands, and in some instances new worlds that they've never returned from.

I wish you the best of success on your journey and am left to thank you for taking the time to read this book. I really appreciate your interest in the existential approach and hope that together we can raise more awareness as to its value for clients in coaching. I believe in the generative effect that existential work can have on our communities and the world at large, one client or coach at a time, and so I would love to hear your thoughts and comments or to connect with you at a future event or online for this purpose.

With love,

References and resources

Core reading (existential coaching)

DeLuca, L. (2008). An exploration of the existential orientation to coaching. Master's thesis. Retrieved from http://repository.upenn.edu/cgi/viewcontent. cgi?article=1008&context=od_theses_msod

Hanaway, M. (2018). *Existential Coaching Skills: The Handbook* (2nd edition). Guernsey: Corporate Harmony.

Jacob, Y.U. (2013). Exploring boundaries of existential coaching. Master's thesis. Retrieved from www.academia.edu/8376861/Exploring_Boundaries_of_ Existential_Coaching

Peltier, B. (2001). The existential stance. In B. Peltier, *The Psychology of Executive Coaching: Theory and Application* (pp. 161–174). New York: Brunner-Routledge.

Spinelli, E. (2010). Existential coaching. In E. Cox, T. Bachkirova & D. Clutterbuck (eds), *The Complete Handbook of Coaching* (pp. 94–106). London: Sage.

van Deurzen, E., & Hanaway, M. (2012). *Existential Perspectives on Coaching.* Basingtoke, UK: Palgrave Macmillan.

Introductions to existentialism

Cooper, M. (2003). *Existential Therapies.* Thousand Oaks, CA: Sage.

Cox, G. (2009). *How to be an Existentialist.* London: Continuum.

Gardiner, P. (2002). *A Very Short Introduction to Kierkegaard.* Oxford: Oxford University Press.

Jacobsen, B. (2007). *Invitation to Existential Psychology.* Chichester, UK: John Wiley & Sons.

Kaufmann, W. (1956). *Existentialism from Dostoyevsky to Sartre.* New York: World.

Panza, C., & Gale, G. (2008). *Existentialism for Dummies.* Chichester, UK: Wiley Publishing Inc.

Olson, R. (1962). *An Introduction to Existentialism.* New York: Dover.

Wartenberg, T.E. (2008). *Existentialism: A Beginner's Guide.* London: Oneworld Publications.

Existential skills

Cohn, H.W. (1997). *Existential Thought and Therapeutic Practice*. London: Sage.

Langdridge, A.D. (2012). Existential coaching psychology: developing a model for effective practice. *The Danish Journal of Coaching Psychology, 2*(1), 83–89.

Spinelli, E., & Horner, C. (2008). Existential approach to coaching psychology. In S. Palmer & A. Whybrow (eds), *Handbook of Coaching Psychology* (pp. 118–132). London: Routledge.

van Deurzen, E., & Adams, M., (2011). *Skills in Existential Counselling & Psychotherapy*. London: Sage.

Yalom, I.D. (1980). *Existential Psychotherapy*. New York: Basic Books.

Yalom, I.D. (2009). *The Gift of Therapy: An Open Letter to a New Generation of Therapists and Their Patients.* New York: Harper Perennial.

Existential happiness

Ivtzan, I., Lomas, T., Worth, P., & Hefferon, K. (2016). *Second Wave Positive Psychology: Embracing the Dark Side of Life*. London: Routledge.

Popovic, N. (2003). Existential anxiety and existential joy. *Practical Philosophy, 5*, 2. Retrieved from http://society-for-philosophy-in-practice.org/journal/pdf/5-2%2032%20Popovic%20-%20Anxiety.pdf

van Deurzen, E. (2008). *Psychotherapy and the Quest for Happiness*. London: Sage.

Wong, P.T.P. (2009). Positive existential psychology. In S. Lopez (ed.), *Encyclopedia*. Oxford: Blackwell. Retrieved from www.drpaulwong.com/existential-positive-psychology

Wong, P.T.P. (2010). What is existential positive psychology. *International Journal of Existential Psychology & Psychotherapy, 3*, 1–10.

Wong, P.T.P. (2011). Positive psychology 2.0: towards a balanced interactive model of the good life. *Canadian Psychology, 52*(2), 69–81.

Wong, P.T.P. (2017). Courage, faith, meaning, and mature happiness in dangerous times. President's Report for the *Positive Living Newsletter* (May). Retrieved from www.icontact-archive.com/wGCjxel7M1K_TfYDgHOt_sggKuLklwVh?w=3

Applied existentialism

Aggerholm, K. (2015). *Talent Development, Existential Philosophy and Sport: On Becoming an Elite Athlete*. London: Routledge.

Hanaway, M. (2019). *The Existential Leader: An Authentic Leader for Our Uncertain Times*. London: Routledge.

Kashdan, T.B. & Biswas-Diener, R. (2014). *The Upside of Your Dark Side*. New York: Hudson Street Press.

Spinelli, E. (1997). *Tales of Unknowing.* London: Duckworth.

van Deurzen, E. (1997). *Everyday Mysteries*. London: Routledge.
Yalom, I.D. (1989). *Love's Executioner & Other Tales of Psychotherapy*. New York: NY: HarperPerennial.

Classic existential literature

Becker, E. (1973/2016). *The Denial of Death*. London: Souvenir Press.
Buber, M. (1937). *I and Thou*. London: Continuum.
Camus, A. (1968). *Lyrical and Critical Essays* (trans. E. C. Kennedy). New York: Knopf.
Frankl, V. (1963). *Man's Search for Meaning*. New York: Pocket Books.
Heidegger, M. (1962). *Being and Time* (trans. J. Macquarrie & E. Robinson). New York: Basic Books.
Kierkegaard, S. (1843/1983). *Fear and Trembling* (trans. H.V. Hong and E.H. Hong). Princeton, NJ: Princeton University Press.
Kierkegaard, S. (1843/1987). *Either/Or* (Vol. II). (trans. H. Hong & E. Hong). Princeton, NJ: Princeton University Press.
May, R. (1950). *The Meaning of Anxiety*. New York: Norton.
May, R. (1981). *Freedom and Destiny*. New York: Norton.
Merleau-Ponty, M. (1962). *The Phenomenology of Perception*. London: Routledge.
Nietzsche, F. (1968). *The Will to Power* (trans. W. Kaufmann & J.R. Hollingdale). New York: Vintage.
Sartre J.P. (1943/1956), *Being and Nothingness: An Essay on Phenomenological Ontology* (trans. H. Barnes). New York: Philosophical Library.
Tillich, P. (1952). *The Courage to Be*. New Haven, CT: Yale University Press.
van Deurzen, E. (2012). *Existential Psychotherapy and Counselling in Practice* (3rd edition). London: Sage. (A long list of suggested further reading – classic literature, novels, plays and a catalogue of sources on psychotherapy – can be found in this book.)

Novels and plays

Becket, S. (1954). *Waiting for Godot: Tragicomedy in Two Acts*. New York: Grove Press.
Bukowski, C. (1962/1994). *Run with the Hunted*. New York: Ecco.
Camus, A. (1942). *The Stranger*. New York: Random House
De Beauvoir, S. (1945). *The Blood of Others*. Paris: Éditions Gallimard.
Dostoevsky, F. (1864/1993). *Notes from the Underground*. New York: Vintage Classics.
Dostoevsky, F. (1869/2004). *The Idiot*. London: Penguin Classics.
Fynn (1974). *Mr God, this is Anna*. Glasgow: William Collins & Co.
Goethe, J.W. von (1774/1989). *The Sorrows of Young Werther*. Harmondsworth, UK: Penguin
Hesse, H. (1924). *Steppenwolf*. New York: Holt.
Kafka, F. (1956). *The Trial*. New York: Vintage

Kafka, F. (1966). *The Metamorphosis*. New York: Norton.
Pirsig, R.M. (1974). *Zen and the Art of Motorcycle Maintenance*. New York: HarperPerennial.
Rice, A. (1976). *Interview with a Vampire*. New York: Ballantine Books.
Sartre, J.P. (1938/1962). *Nausea*. Harmondsworth, UK: Penguin.
Sartre, J.P. (1989). *No Exit and Three Other Plays*. New York: Vintage.
Shakespeare, W. (1603/1991). *Hamlet*. New York: AMS Press.
Tolstoy, L. (1868, 2004). *The Death of Ivan Ilych*. New York: Barnes and Noble Books.
Yalom, I.D. (1992). *When Nietzsche Wept: A Novel of Obsession*. New York: HarperPerennial.

Existentialism in business

Agapitou, V., & Bourantas, D. (2017). *Existential Intelligence and Strategic Leadership*. Lap Lambert Academic Publishing.
Agarwal, J., & Malloy, D.C. (2000). The role of existentialism in ethical business decision-making. *Business Ethics: A European Review, 9*, 143–154.
Boje, D.M. (2001). Existential leadership. Retrieved from https://business.nmsu.edu/~dboje/teaching/338/existential_leadership.htm
Brown, B. (2012). *Daring Greatly: How the Courage to Be Vulnerable Transforms the Way We Live, Love, Parent, and Lead*. New York: Gotham Books.
Brown, B. (2012). Leadership manifesto. Retrieved from https://brenebrown.com/wp-content/uploads/2013/09/DaringGreatly-LeadershipManifesto-8x10.pdf
Brown, B. (2013). *The Power of Vulnerability: Teachings of Authenticity, Connections and Courage*. Louisville, KY: Sounds True.
D'Souza, S., & Renner, D. (2014). *Not Knowing: The Art of Turning Uncertainty into Opportunity*. London: Lid Publishing.
Friedman, S.D. (2014). *Total Leadership: Be a Better Leader, Have a Richer Life*. Boston, MA: Harvard Business Publishing.
Goffee, R., & Jones, J. (2005). Managing authenticity: The paradox of great leadership. *Harvard Business Review, 85*, 86–94.
Hanaway, H. (2018). *Existential Leadership*. Guernsey: Corporate Harmony.
Hanaway, M. (2019). *The Existential Leader: An Authentic Leader for Our Uncertain Times*. London: Routledge.
Heifetz, R.A., & Linsky, M. (2002). *Leadership on the Line: Staying Alive through the dangers of leading*. Boston, MA: Harvard Business School Press.
Herrmann, A.F. (2011). Existentialism and the development of leaders. Paper presented at the Central States Communication Association Convention, Milwaukee, WI, March 2011. Retrieved from www.academia.edu/4070013/Existentialism_and_the_Development_of_Leaders
Hill, L.A. (2003). *Becoming a Manager: How New Managers Master the Challenges of Leadership* (2nd edition). Boston, MA: Harvard Business School Press.
Hill, L.A., & Lineback, K. (2011). *Being the Boss: The 3 Imperatives for becoming a Great Leader*. Boston, MA: Harvard Business Review Press.

Hill, L.A., Brandeau, G., Truelove, E. & Lineback, K. (2014). Collective genius. *Harvard Business Review*, *92*(6), 94–102.

Hill, L.A., Brandeau, G., Truelove, E., & Lineback, K. (2014). *Collective Genius: The Art and Practice of Leading Innovation*. Boston, MA: Harvard Business Review Press.

Horner, C. (2011). A hazy notion. *Coaching at Work*, *6*(5), 38–41. Retrieved from www.coaching-at-work.com/coaching-at-work-volume-6-issue-5-page-38/

Jopling, A. (2012). Coaching leaders from an existential perspective. In E. van Deurzen & M. Hanaway (eds), *Existential Perspectives on Coaching*. Basingstoke, UK: Palgrave Macmillan.

Kelly, L. (1998). *An Existential Systems Approach to Managing Organizations*. Westport, CT: Quorum Books.

Ketola, T. (2008). A holistic corporate responsibility model: Integrating values, discourses and actions. *Journal of Business Ethics*, *80*(3), 419–435.

Khan, A. (1994). Kierkegaard on authority and leadership: Political logic in religious thought. *Sophia*, *33*(3), 74–88.

Laloux, F. (2014). *Reinventing Organisations – A Guide to Creating Organisations Inspired by the Next Stage of Human Consciousness*. Brussels, Belgium: Nelson Parker.

Längle, A., & Bürgi, D. (2014). *Existentielles Coaching: Theoretische Orientierung, Grundlagen und Praxis für Coaching, Organisationsberatung und Supervision*. Vienna: Facultas Universitätsverlag.

Lawler, J. (2005). The essence of leadership? Existentialism and leadership. *Leadership*, *1*, 215–231.

LeBon, T., & Arnaud, D. (2012). Existential coaching and major life decisions. In E. van Deurzen & M. Hanaway (eds). *Existential Perspectives on Coaching*. Basingstoke, UK: Palgrave Macmillan.

Lipman-Blumen, J. (2000). *Connective Leadership*. Oxford: Oxford University Press.

Luthans, F., & Aviolo, B.J. (2003). Authentic leadership: A positive-developmental approach. In K.S. Cameron, J.E. Dutton & R.E. Quinn (eds), *Positive Organisational Leadership* (pp. 241–264). San Francisco, CA: Barret-Kohler.

Mengel, T. (2008). Leading with 'emotional intelligence' – existential and motivational analysis in leadership and leadership development. *i-Manager's Journal on Educational Psychology*, *5*(4), 24–31.

Nietzsche, Friedrich (1967/1888). *The Will to Power* (trans. Walter Kaufmann & R. J. Hollingdale). New York: Vintage Books. [Source for the Superman & Superwoman theory of leadership.]

Obolenski, N. (2010). *Complex Adaptive Leadership: Getting Chaos and Complexity to work*. London: Gower. Available online at www.gpmfirst.com/books/complex-adaptive-leadership.

Ogilvy, J. (2003). What coaches can learn from Sartre. *Strategy and Business*, *33*, 39–47.

Pruzan, P. (2008). Spiritual-based leadership in business. *Journal of Human Values*, *14*(2), 101–114.

Sinek, S. (2011). *Start with Why: How Great Leaders Inspire Everyone to Take Action.* London: Penguin Books.

Sinek, S. (2014). *Leaders Eat Last: Why Some Teams Pull Together and Others Don't.* New York: Portfolio/Penguin.

Starlit, B. (2013). Kierkegaard and authentic leadership. Retrieved from www.stagisblog.com/Blog/2013/02/kierkegaard-and-authentic-leadership.

Storsletten, V.M.L., & Jakobsen, O.D. (2014). Development of leadership theory in the perspective of Kierkegaard's philosophy. *Journal of Business Ethics*, *128*(2), 337–349. Retrieved from https://core.ac.uk/download/pdf/52082941.pdf

Coaching foundations

Bird, J., & Gornall S. (2016). *The Art of Coaching: A Handbook of Tips and Tools.* Routledge: New York.

Bolton, N. (2017). Foundations. Unpublished manuscript. London: Animas Centre for Coaching.

De Haan, E. (2008), *Relational Coaching: Journeys towards Mastering One-to-One Learning.* Chichester, UK: John Wiley.

Kline, N. (2011). *Time to Think: Listening to Ignite the Human Mind.* London: Octopus Publishing Book.

Palmer, S., & Whybrow, A. (2007). *Handbook of Coaching Psychology.* Hove, UK: Routledge.

Van Nieuwerburgh, C. (2017). *An Introduction to Coaching Skills: A Practical Guide* (2nd edition). London: Sage.

Van Oudtshoorn, M. (2006). *A Framework for Coaching.* London: i-coachacademy.

Ontological coaching

Castillo Noriega, M., & Romero Coloma, M. (2016). Regaining leadership through ontological coaching for female EFL instructors. Retrieved from www.academia.edu/33397010/Title_Regaining_Leadership_through_Ontological_Coaching_for_Female_EFL_Instructors_Author

Shabi, A. (2015). Ontological coaching. Unpublished manuscript. Retrieved from www.talkingabout.com.au/PDF/AboodiShabiOntologicalCoaching.pdf

Sieler, A. (2003). *Coaching to the Human Soul: Ontological Coaching and Deep Change, Vol. I.* Melbourne: Newfield-Australia.

Sieler, A. (2007). *Coaching to the Human Soul: Ontological Coaching and Deep Change, Vol. II.* Melbourne: Newfield-Australia.

Sieler, A. (2012). *Coaching to the Human Soul: Ontological Coaching and Deep Change, Vol. III.* Melbourne: Newfield Institute.

Sieler, A. (2011). Ontological Coaching. In E. Cox, T. Bachkirova & D. Clutterbuck. (eds), *The Complete Handbook of Coaching* (pp. 107–119). London: Sage. Available from: www.linkedin.com/pulse/chapter-ontological-coaching-alan-sieler/

Getting clients

Chandler, S., & Litvin, S. (2013). *The Prosperous Coach*. Anna maria, FL: Maurice Basset.

Brown-Volkman, D. (2003). *Four Steps to Building a Profitable Coaching Practice: A Complete Marketing Resource Guide for Coaches*. Lincoln, NE: iUniverse.

Cardone, G. (2012). *Sell or Be Sold: How to Get Your Way in Business and in Life*. Austin, TX: Greenleaf Book Group Press.

Cornelius, C. (2013). *One in Ten. How to Survive Your First Ten Years in Business*. Compton: Appletree Publications.

Fairley, S.G., & Stout, C.E. (2004). *Getting Started in Personal and Executive Coaching*. New Jersey, NJ: John Wiley & Sons.

Godin, S. (2005). *Purple Cow: Transform your Business by Being Remarkable*. London: Penguin Books.

Hayden, C.J. (2013). *Get clients Now!: A 28-Day Marketing Program for Professionals, Consultants, and Coaches*. New York: Amacom.

Ries, A., & Trout, J. (2001). *Positioning: The Battle for Your Mind*. New York: McGraw-Hill

Ries, A., & Trout, J. (1994). *The 22 Immutable Laws of Marketing*. New York: Harper Business.

Vaynerchuk, G. (2018). *Crushing It!: How Great Entrepreneurs Build Their Business and Influence – and How You Can, Too*. New York: Harper Business.

Training opportunities

www.nspc.org.uk

Full MA Existential Coaching

http://acecoaching.eu/en/training/existential-coaching

18 days of training in 7 blocks + supervision

www.existential.coach

Weekend courses in existential coaching, 1:1 coach training and existential coaching supervision

www.i-coachacademy.com

Coaching training with existential underpinnings

www.animascoaching.com

Certificate in transformational coaching (underpinned by some existential principles)

www.newfieldinstitute.com.au

Certified ontological coaching and leadership program

Other resources and online materials

Shots of Awe with Jason Silva

www.youtube.com/channel/UClYb9NpXnRemxYoWbcYANsA

Philosophical espresso from Jason Silva, philosopher and filmmaker with a positive existential attitude and an appetite to think deeply about contemporary issues such as technology, relationships and meaning in a fast pace digitalised world.
Recommended:

www.youtube.com/watch?v=Yb-OYmHVchQ (Existential Bummer)

www.youtube.com/watch?v=CWrHCCYgGSQ (How We Free Ourselves of Existential Panic)

Existential Comics

http://existentialcomics.com

Short cartoon depicting the human condition in all its forms filled with references to famous philosophers and including explanations for some of the more complex and difficult to understand jokes linked to specific philosophical concepts.

Yannick's Existential Nuggets

www.coachingandmediation.net/existential-nuggets/

Lots of illustrations of how existential themes show up in everyday life with a short paragraph on how each is relevant in the context of coaching and philosophy.

Cartoon wisdom

www.youtube.com/watch?v=de2grEPn7rg

Analysis of the cartoon Rick & Morty, during which its creator Dan Harmon talks about its existential themes, especially meaninglessness and absurdity. The whole series is packed with references to existential philosophy.

Another great resource if you are into contemporary culture is the YouTube channel Wise Crack (www.youtube.com/channel/UC6-ymYjG0SU0jUWnWh9ZzEQ), which is packed with references and explanations of existential and other philosophy and presented in a modern format.

Daytripper – Graphic novel

www.vertigocomics.com/graphic-novels/daytripper-2010/daytripper

A beautifully drawn illustration of some of the big questions in life. As you read through the novel, which tells episodes from the main character's life in a non-linear fashion, you get used to the idea of death being an inevitable part of life which encourages the reader to appreciate living in a new way.

Kim Kierkegaardashian

https://twitter.com/KimKierkegaard

This Twitter feed combines tweets from Kim Kardashian and Soren Kierkegaard – Many LOLs!

Being in the World – a philosophy documentary

www.youtube.com/watch?v=k5QJ8s3qUyA

Ontology explained through the lens of jazz, carpentry and flamenco, beautifully illustrated by filmmaker Tao Ruspoli.

Lecture series: No Excuses: Existentialism and the Meaning of Life

https://mobile.audible.co.uk/pd/No-Excuses-Existentialism-and-the-Meaning-of-Life-Audiobook/B00DDYKAE6

Robert C. Solomon's series of lectures and audio material introducing a range of existential thought.

Movies and shows

I ♥ Huckabees (2004)

Existential comedy about a couple of private detectives hired to investigate the meaning of the life of their clients.

The Matrix (1999)

Choosing to face a cruel reality rather than remaining in a safe illusion.

Fight Club (1999)

Hitting rock bottom and facing the pain in order to find meaning and live fully.

Inception (2010)

Questioning the nature of reality and free will.

Interview with the Vampire (1994)

How to find meaning in an existence that has no defined ending.

Seven Samurai (1954)

Living in accordance with your values no matter the odds.

Superbad (2007)

A story about creating yourself.

Stranger than Fiction (2006)

Part romantic comedy, part absurd fantasy.

Dave Made a Maze (2017)

A group of people enter an absurd world to find their friend.

Black Mirror (2011–)

A mirror into the darkest parts of human nature.

The Walking Dead (2010–)

A range of characters choose to either cling to their former reality and values or reinvent themselves in the face of daily encounters with death.

Rick & Morty (2013–)

In a world of multidimensional space travel, where anything that could exist, will exist, what matters?

The Truman Show (1998)

What if your life was an illusion and then you find out?

Blade Runner (1982/2017)

What does it mean to be human in a world where people are tired and flat emotionally while robots live with youthful energy in the face of their 4-year life space.

Westworld (2016–)

What makes us human in a world where artificial intelligence has developed consciousness and attachment?

Happyish (2015)

How can we be happy stuck in the mundane struggle of everyday living?

Apocalypse Now (1979)

How far are you willing to go to create yourself, live authentically and exert your freedom?

The Seventh Seal (1957)

Does god exist? Is life meaningful without?

Flight from Death: The Quest for Immortality (2003)

Documentary, self-explanatory.

Waking Life (2001)

Somewhere between dreaming and waking there is a space for deep reflection and asking all the questions, with a special section specifically about existentialism.

Ready Player One (2018)

In the future most people spend their waking time in a virtual reality, where they can be whoever they like, to avoid the meaninglessness of their existence.

Existentialism-for-all project

Do you know any more? Would you add others?
Support my project to spread the existential word!

The above resources are by no means exhaustive or complete. A growing selection of online resources started by me and grown by you can be found at:

www.existential.coach/thisisexistential

Be a part of this project! My aim is for as many people as possible to better understand their human condition as to live fuller, richer and more considered lives. Therefore I am continuously looking for literature, arts and culture that illustrates existential philosophy as it emerges in everyday living by means of stories, books, plays, movies, graphic novels, YouTube videos, song lyrics, poems, cartoons, public social media posts, memes . . . anything goes!

In order for everybody to be able to be a part of this I've created a public document that anybody can add to and over time I hope to build a large database of resources to help people grasp why existentialism is still relevant today (and without having to work through the dense philosophical texts, but with the hope that many will choose to do so further down the line).

Your help will be very much appreciated as I very much believe in bottom-up approaches. Thank you!

Index

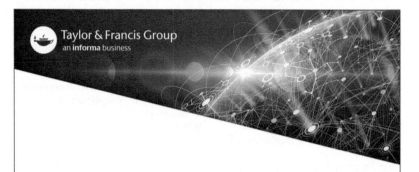